guidance   understandi

peace   generous   trust

disappointments   obedi

respect   solid   worship

e resting   serve   riches

thers   money   worry

LETTERS from GOD

for teens

God's Promises for You

Honor Books
Tulsa, Oklahoma

Letters from God for Teens

ISBN 1-56292-711-6
Copyright © 2000 by GRQ Ink, Inc.
1948 Green Hills Boulevard
Franklin, Tennessee 37067

Published by **Honor Books**
P.O. Box 55388
Tulsa, Oklahoma 74155

Developed by GRQ Ink, Inc.
Manuscript written by Melody Carlson
Cover design, interior design, and composition by
Whisner Design Group, Tulsa, Oklahoma

Dear Friend,

Do you long for a friend who's always there for you? Do you wish you had someone you could really talk to—day or night—someone who's never too busy to listen? Someone who knows every single little thing about you but loves you just the same?

That is who I am. And I am here for you, ready and eager to listen. I understand everything you're going through. And I know everywhere you've been. I even know what lies ahead. I have some very helpful advice for you, and I want to be your best friend.

All My love,

Your Heavenly Father

REVELATION 3:20 NIV

Here I am! I stand at the door and knock. If anyone hears my voice and opens the door, I will come in.

Contents

Forever Love

Dear Friend,

Your heart is like a dry sponge. Whether you can admit it or not, you long for love the way a man lost in the desert longs for cool water.

I have watched you search for love in all sorts of places. In your family, school, friends. While you may find bits and pieces of love along the way, it is never enough, is it? The love you stumble across never fully satisfies your deep inner longing, because you long for real love, constant love, perfect love. You long for My love.

That's because only My love can quench your thirsting heart. For that's the way I made you—with a space inside that only I can fill. The love I have for you is perfect, complete, and forever. And it is all you will ever need.

All My love,

Your Loving Father

PSALM 42:8 TLB

Day by day the Lord also pours out his steadfast love upon me, and through the night I sing his songs and pray to God who gives me life.

> **I love them that love me; and those that seek me early shall find me.**
>
> PROVERBS 8:17 KJV

God, who is rich in mercy, because of His great love with which He loved us, even when we were dead in trespasses, made us alive together with Christ (by grace you have been saved).
EPHESIANS 2:4-5 NKJV

To all of you in Rome whom God loves and has called to be his holy people: Grace and peace to you from God our Father and the Lord Jesus Christ.
ROMANS 1:7 NCV

ROMANS 5:8 NRSV

God proves his love for us in that while we were still sinners Christ died for us.

So you see, our love for him comes as a result of his loving us first.
1 JOHN 4:19 TLB

The Father Himself loves you, since you have loved Me and have believed that I came from the Father.
JOHN 16:27 MLB

Delight yourself in the LORD and he will give you the desires of your heart.
PSALM 37:4 NIV

Love

Forever Love

> **"O Lord, God of Israel, there is no God like you in heaven or on earth—you who keep your covenant of love with your servants who continue wholeheartedly in your way."**
>
> 2 CHRONICLES 6:14 NIV

I am convinced that nothing can ever separate us from his love. Death can't, and life can't. The angels won't, and all the powers of hell itself cannot keep God's love away.
ROMANS 8:38 TLB

You should know that the Lord your God, He is the only God; the faithful God, keeping His covenant and showing loving kindness to a thousand generations of those who love Him and are obedient to his orders.
DEUTERONOMY 7:9 MLB

I trust in your unfailing love; my heart rejoices in your salvation.
PSALM 13:5 NIV

Let your steadfast love, O Lord, be upon us, even as we hope in you.
PSALM 33:22 NRSV

"Stay always within the boundaries where God's love can reach and bless you. Wait patiently for the eternal life that our Lord Jesus Christ in his mercy is going to give you."

JUDE 21 TLB

Hope does not disappoint us, because God's love has been poured into our hearts through the Holy Spirit that has been given to us.
ROMANS 5:5 NRSV

JEREMIAH 31:3 TLB

Long ago the Lord had said to Israel: I have loved you, O my people, with an everlasting love; with loving-kindness I have drawn you to me.

I will be glad and rejoice in your love, for you saw my affliction and knew the anguish of my soul.
PSALM 31:7 NIV

I am confident of this, that the one who began a good work among you will bring it to completion by the day of Jesus Christ.
PHILIPPIANS 1:6 NRSV

May the Lord lead your hearts into God's love and Christ's patience.
2 THESSALONIANS 3:5 NCV

We have known and believe the love that God has for us. God is love, and those who abide in love abide in God, and God abides in them.
1 JOHN 4:16 NRSV

Love

Incredible Power

My Own,

Oh, if only you knew what power you can access through Me and what strength and might are available to you if you'd only ask. But so often you don't ask. You forget, you're afraid, you think you're undeserving. You may even doubt My willingness to help. But I want you to know that My power, My might, My strength is there for you when you need it. Power to help you face your problems and overcome them. Power to love beyond your human limitations. Power to do what is right, even when you must stand alone. Power to be all that I have called you to be.

I know you have needs. I know about your weaknesses. I know that you can't overcome all the obstacles in your life without My help. That's why I've made My own power and might available to you. So when you feel weak, call on Me, and I will add My strength to yours. When you feel powerless, come to Me, and I will empower you to overcome any obstacle. When you feel outnumbered, count on Me, and I, Almighty God, will stand beside you. Just ask. It's that simple.

In power and might,

The Almighty God

PSALM 81:1 NIV

Sing for joy to God our strength; shout aloud to the God of Jacob!

❝God has not given us a spirit of fear, but of power and of love and of a sound mind.❞

2 TIMOTHY 1:7 NKJV

So that you will walk in a manner worthy of the Lord, to please Him in all respects, bearing fruit in every good work and increasing in the knowledge of God; strengthened with all power, according to His glorious might, for the attaining of all steadfastness and patience; joyously giving thanks to the Father, who has qualified us to share in the inheritance of the saints in Light.

COLOSSIANS 1:10-12 NAS

PSALM 68:34 NIV
Proclaim the power of God, whose majesty is over Israel, whose power is in the skies.

Wealth and honor come from you; you are the ruler of all things. In your hands are strength and power to exalt and give strength to all. Now, our God, we give you thanks, and praise your glorious name.

1 CHRONICLES 29:12-13 NIV

Consequently, all the nations of the earth will know that the hand of the Lord is mighty, and you will revere the Lord your God always.

JOSHUA 4:24 MLB

Power

> **" I will teach you about the power of God; the ways of the Almighty I will not conceal. "**
>
> JOB 27:11 NIV

So that your faith might rest not on human wisdom but on the power of God.
1 CORINTHIANS 2:5 NRSV

Proclaim the power of God,
whose majesty is over Israel,
whose power is in the skies.
PSALM 68:34 NIV

O LORD, be gracious to us; we long for you.
Be our strength every morning,
our salvation in time of distress.
ISAIAH 33:2 NIV

I am not ashamed of the gospel, for it is the power of God for salvation to everyone who believes, to the Jew first and also to the Greek.
ROMANS 1:16 NAS

The LORD is my strength and my song;
he has become my salvation.
He is my God, and I will praise him,
my father's God, and I will exalt him.
EXODUS 15:2 NIV

Jesus has the power of God, by which he has given us everything we need to live and to serve God. We have these things because we know him. Jesus called us by his glory and goodness.
2 PETER 1:3 NCV

❝I love you, O LORD, my strength.❞

PSALM 18:1 NIV

I said, "I have toiled in vain, I have spent My strength for nothing and vanity; yet surely the justice due to Me is with the LORD, and My reward with My God." And now says the LORD, who formed Me from the womb to be His Servant, to bring Jacob back to Him, so that Israel might be gathered to Him (for I am honored in the sight of the LORD, and My God is My strength).
ISAIAH 49:4-5 NAS

ISAIAH 33:2 NIV
O LORD, be gracious to us; we long for you. Be our strength every morning, our salvation in time of distress.

Praise the Lord, you angels of his; praise his glory and his strength.
PSALM 29:1 TLB

Whom have I in heaven but You? And there is none upon earth that I desire besides You. My flesh and my heart fail; But God is the strength of my heart and my portion forever.
PSALM 73:25-26 NKJV

The Sovereign LORD is my strength; he makes my feet like the feet of a deer, he enables me to go on the heights.
HABAKKUK 3:19 NIV

Power

Ultimate Understanding

Dear Friend,

So many times you have thought, No one understands me. But believe Me, I do. I understand you completely—even better than you understand yourself.

I understand you from the inside out. I'm aware of every little chromosome in your genetic makeup (just as I have known each and every one of your ancestors). And I know and understand exactly what your life is like. I know that you often struggle with family, friends, even your very own heart.

I understand that your life isn't always easy. No one's is. But like soft warm blankets, My compassion and understanding are wrapped all around you. And I am determined to see you through the confusion and frustration of your day-to-day life. I do understand you, and if you let Me, I'll teach you to understand yourself.

With wisdom and love,

Your Heavenly Father

JAMES 1:5 NIV

If any of you lacks wisdom, he should ask God, who gives generously to all without finding fault, and it will be given to him.

> **Trust in the LORD
> with all your heart
> and do not lean on
> your own understanding.
> In all your ways acknowledge Him,
> and He will make
> your paths straight.**

PROVERBS 3:5-6 NAS

We know that the Son of God has come and has given us an understanding, that we may know Him who is true; and we are in Him who is true, in His Son Jesus Christ. This is the true God and eternal life.
1 JOHN 5:20 NKJV

PSALM 119:34 NAS

Give me understanding, that I may observe Your law, and keep it with all my heart.

Yes, God's riches are very great, and his wisdom and knowledge have no end! No one can explain the things God decides or understand his ways.
ROMANS 11:33 NCV

God, who said, "Let there be light in the darkness," has made us understand that this light is the brightness of the glory of God that is seen in the face of Jesus Christ.
2 CORINTHIANS 4:6 NLT

The secret things belong to the LORD our God, but the revealed things belong to us and to our children forever, to observe all the words of this law.
DEUTERONOMY 29:29 NRSV

Understanding

> **"Give me understanding,
> that I may observe Your law,
> and keep it with all my heart. "**
>
> PSALM 119:34 NAS

Your hands made me and formed me;
give me understanding to learn your
commands.
PSALM 119:73 NIV

A wise man will hear and increase in
learning, and a man of understanding will
acquire wise counsel.
PROVERBS 1:5 NAS

Is not wisdom found among the aged?
Does not long life bring understanding?
"To God belong wisdom and power;
counsel and understanding are his."
JOB 12:12-13 NIV

Lead me in Your truth and teach me,
for You are the God of my salvation;
for You I wait all the day.
PSALM 25:5 NAS

My child, be attentive to my wisdom;
incline your ear to my understanding.
PROVERBS 5:1 NRSV

May the LORD give you wisdom and
understanding, and give you charge
concerning Israel, that you may keep the
law of the LORD your God.
1 CHRONICLES 22:12 NKJV

> **Direct me in the path of your commands, for there I find delight.**
>
> PSALM 119:35 NIV

Have you never heard or understood? Don't you know that the LORD is the everlasting God, the Creator of all the earth? He never grows faint or weary. No one can measure the depths of his understanding.
ISAIAH 40:28 NLT

Wisdom calls to you like someone shouting; understanding raises her voice.
PROVERBS 8:1 NCV

PSALM 119:130
NRSV
The unfolding of your words gives light; it imparts understanding to the simple.

If you call out for insight and cry aloud for understanding, ...then you will understand the fear of the LORD and find the knowledge of God.
PROVERBS 2:3-5 NIV

The Spirit of the Lord shall rest upon Him, the Spirit of wisdom and understanding, the Spirit of counsel and might, the Spirit of knowledge and of the fear of the Lord.
ISAIAH 11:2 NKJV

Understanding

Guidance for the Way

Dear Searching One,

You have so many choices to make in your life. Small daily decisions—not to mention those huge life decisions, like what you will do after graduation day—can wear you down. I know that sometimes you feel overwhelmed.

But I am here, My friend, ready to give you wisdom, insight, and direction. I know where you've been, and I know what lies ahead. And because I love you, I long to help you make choices that lead to success and happiness. All you have to do is ask.

But don't expect that I will always write My answers across the sky or speak to you in a voice of thunder. Most often, you will hear My voice in the quiet stillness of your own heart. Ask Me for wisdom and listen for My voice. As you do, My peace will follow you wherever you go.

Longing to lead,

Your Shepherd

PROVERBS 3:6 NKJV

In all your ways
acknowledge Him, and He
shall direct your paths.

"I will instruct you and teach you in the way you should go; I will counsel you and watch over you."

PSALM 32:8 NIV

Don't copy the behavior and customs of this world, but be a new and different person with a fresh newness in all you do and think. Then you will learn from your own experience how his ways will really satisfy you.
ROMANS 12:2 TLB

Your ears will hear a word behind you, "This is the way, walk in it," whenever you turn to the right or to the left.
ISAIAH 30:21 NAS

PROVERBS 6:22 TLB

Every day and all night long their counsel will lead you and save you from harm; when you wake up in the morning, let their instructions guide you into the new day.

The LORD will always lead you. He will satisfy your needs in dry lands and give strength to your bones. You will be like a garden that has much water, like a spring that never runs dry.
ISAIAH 58:11 NCV

This God is our God forever and ever. He will guide us from now on.
PSALM 48:14 NCV

Direction

Total Forgiveness

Dear Friend,

I know exactly how many times you've blown it. I've seen you get discouraged and angry and frustrated. I've heard you say things you didn't really mean. I know about your mistakes and even the secrets of your heart. Yet, do you realize that, no matter what you do, I will always love you?

And because I love you, I've made a way to erase your mistakes and cleanse your heart from sin. I sent My very own Son, Jesus Christ, to take the punishment for your sin and rebellion. I allowed Him to die in your place so you can live forever.

Bring your broken and troubled heart to Me. Bring your blunders and mistakes, your failures and shortcomings. Bring them all to Me. I will cleanse and restore you. I will make you whole again. I will wash you with the miracle of forgiveness and heal you with the power of My love.

With mercy,

Your Forgiving Father

I JOHN 1:9 KJV

If we confess our sins, he is faithful and just to forgive us our sins, and to cleanse us from all unrighteousness.

"If anyone is in Christ, there is a new creation: everything old has passed away; see, everything has become new!"

2 CORINTHIANS 5:17 NRSV

I, yes, I alone am He who blots away your sins for my own sake and will never think of them again.
ISAIAH 43:25 TLB

In Him we enjoy redemption through His blood, the forgiveness of our trespasses to the measure of the wealth of His grace.
EPHESIANS 1:7 MLB

PSALM 103:12 NKJV

As far as the east is from the west, so far has He removed our transgressions from us.

I say: Love your enemies! Pray for those who persecute you! In that way you will be acting as true sons of your Father in heaven. For he gives his sunlight to both the evil and the good, and sends rain on the just and on the unjust too.
MATTHEW 5:44-45 TLB

"People will no longer have to teach their neighbors and relatives to know the LORD, because all people will know me, from the least to the most important," says the LORD. "I will forgive them for the wicked things they did, and I will not remember their sins anymore."
JEREMIAH 31:34 NCV

Forgiveness

> **"When you stand praying, if you hold anything against anyone, forgive him, so that your Father in heaven may forgive you your sins."**
>
> MARK 11:25 NIV

I will be merciful to them in their wrongdoings, and I will remember their sins no more.
HEBREWS 8:12 TLB

Come back to me, you unfaithful children, and I will forgive you for being unfaithful.
Yes, we will come to you,
because you are the LORD our God.
JEREMIAH 3:22 NCV

Your heavenly Father will forgive you if you forgive those who sin against you; but if you refuse to forgive them, he will not forgive you.
MATTHEW 6:14-15 TLB

You will remember your sins and cover your mouth in silence and shame when I forgive you of all that you have done, says the Sovereign LORD.
EZEKIEL 16:63 NLT

Truly, Thou, O LORD, art good and ready to forgive, rich in lovingkindness to all who call on Thee.
PSALM 86:5 MLB

The LORD is near to the brokenhearted, and saves the crushed in spirit.
PSALM 34:18 NRSV

> **"You have forgiven the iniquity of Your people; you have covered all their sin."**
>
> PSALM 85:2 NKJV

My mercy I will keep for him forever, and My covenant shall stand firm with him.

PSALM 89:28 NKJV

I will be his Father, and he shall be My son; and I will not take My mercy away from him, as I took it from him who was before you.

1 CHRONICLES 17:13 NKJV

MALACHI 3:6 TLB

I am the Lord—I do not change. That is why you are not already utterly destroyed [for my mercy endures forever].

Love your enemies, do good to them, and lend to them without expecting to get anything back. Then your reward will be great, and you will be sons of the Most High, because he is kind to the ungrateful and wicked. Be merciful, just as your Father is merciful. Do not judge, and you will not be judged. Do not condemn, and you will not be condemned. Forgive, and you will be forgiven. Give, and it will be given to you. A good measure, pressed down, shaken together and running over, will be poured into your lap. For with the measure you use, it will be measured to you.

LUKE 6:35-38 NIV

Forgiveness

My plans for you are totally amazing.

Awesome Plan

My Own,

Sometimes you wonder what kind of difference your one solitary life can make on this great planet that all My creation shares. And I can understand how that might overwhelm you at times. But I want you to know I have great plans for you. I have plans that you cannot begin to imagine, plans that will touch and impact the lives of others, plans that will transform you into a person who thinks as I do.

Just like an earthly father dreams of the things his child might grow up to do and be, I dream for you. My dreams, though amazing, are dreams that really can come true. But I need your cooperation. I need you to come to Me, to learn from Me, and to walk in My ways. Oh what marvelous things we can accomplish together!

Planning for big things,

Your Loving Father

PROVERBS 16:1,3 NCV

People may make plans in their minds, but only the LORD can make them come true.... Depend on the LORD in whatever you do, and your plans will succeed.

"I know the plans I have for you," declares the LORD, "plans to prosper you and not to harm you, plans to give you hope and a future."

JEREMIAH 29:11 NIV

When the Holy Spirit, who is truth, comes, he shall guide you into all truth, for he will not be presenting his own ideas, but will be passing on to you what he has heard. He will tell you about the future.
JOHN 16:13 TLB

ISAIAH 14:26 TLB

This is my plan for the whole earth—I will do it by my mighty power that reaches everywhere around the world.

Delight yourself also in the LORD, and He shall give you the desires of your heart.
PSALM 37:4 NKJV

"There is hope for your future," declares the LORD, "and your children will return to their own territory."
JEREMIAH 31:17 NAS

Lead me in the path of your commands, because that makes me happy.
PSALM 119:35 NCV

Your beginnings will seem humble, so prosperous will your future be.
JOB 8:7 NIV

The Future

Complete Acceptance

My Treasured One,

How many times you have cried out for acceptance! Believe Me, I know how much you want to be loved for who you are. Even in the still of the night, I have heard your silent cries, and I have reached out for you in love.

For I do accept you, My beloved, just as you are. To Me, you are uniquely beautiful and wonderfully grand. I know because I made you. Did you know that I designed everything about you when you were smaller than a snowflake? You are my most magnificent creation.

Oh, I know you make mistakes and you still have a lot of growing to do. But I am pleased that you are searching for truth. I am glad that you are looking to Me. And I know you sometimes question why I made you the way I did. But I have My reasons. Just trust Me. And know this: I love and accept you, right now, just the way you are!

With complete acceptance,

Your Father God

JEREMIAH 31:3 KJV

The LORD hath appeared of old unto me, saying, Yea, I have loved thee with an everlasting love: therefore with lovingkindness have I drawn thee.

> ❝ **To all who received him, who believed in his name, he gave power to become children of God.** ❞
>
> JOHN 1:12 NRSV

God so loved the world, that he gave his only begotten Son, that whosoever believeth in Him should not perish, but have everlasting life.
JOHN 3:16 KJV

What can we ever say to such wonderful things as these? If God is on our side, who can ever be against us?
ROMANS 8:31 TLB

HEBREWS 4:16 NRSV

Let us therefore approach the throne of grace with boldness, so that we may receive mercy and find grace to help in time of need.

There is now no condemnation awaiting those who belong to Christ Jesus.
ROMANS 8:1 TLB

It is by grace you have been saved, through faith—and this not from yourselves, it is the gift of God—not by works, so that no one can boast. For we are God's workmanship, created in Christ Jesus to do good works, which God prepared in advance for us to do.
EPHESIANS 2:8-10 NIV

Acceptance

> **The LORD is good to everyone. He showers compassion on all his creation.**
>
> PSALM 145:9 NLT

Yes, all have sinned; all fall short of God's glorious ideal; yet now God declares us "not guilty" of offending him if we trust in Jesus Christ, who in his kindness freely takes away our sins.
ROMANS 3:23-24 TLB

Let the words of my mouth and the meditation of my heart be acceptable to you, O LORD, my rock and my redeemer.
PSALM 19:14 NRSV

God, be merciful to me because you are loving. Because you are always ready to be merciful, wipe out all my wrongs.
PSALM 51:1 NCV

Through your faith in Christ Jesus you are all sons of God. As many of you as have been baptized into Christ have clothed yourselves with Christ. There is neither Jew nor Greek, there is neither slave nor freeman, there is neither male nor female, because you are all one in Christ Jesus.
GALATIANS 3:26-28 MLB

66 The Lord our God is merciful and forgiving, even though we have rebelled against him. 99

DANIEL 9:9 NIV

In your great mercy you did not put an end to them or abandon them, for you are a gracious and merciful God.
NEHEMIAH 9:31 NIV

Has God forgotten to be gracious? or has He in anger withdrawn His compassion?
PSALM 77:9 NAS

DEUTERONOMY 4:31 TLB

The Lord your God is merciful—he will not abandon you nor destroy you nor forget the promises he has made to your ancestors.

I will tell of the kindnesses of the LORD, the deeds for which he is to be praised, according to all the LORD has done for us—yes, the many good things he has done for the house of Israel, according to his compassion and many kindnesses.
ISAIAH 63:7 NIV

He had to be made like His brethren in all things, so that He might become a merciful and faithful high priest in things pertaining to God, to make propitiation for the sins of the people.
HEBREWS 2:17 NAS

Acceptance

Amazing Peace

My Own,

When things get unbearably hectic, do you ever long for "a little peace in your life"? Perhaps you imagine going away to some tranquil spot, like a sunny beach on a deserted island where all you can hear is the gentle lapping of the waves along the sand. Yes, that's one kind of peace. But it's a temporary one.

The peace I give you can endure throughout the most turbulent and trying times. It can carry you through the thick of the battle and leave you with the certainty that I am still in control of your life. When everything else is falling apart, My peace offers you the assurance that I am still holding your hand.

The world doesn't understand My peace; for My peace doesn't always force soldiers to lay down their arms. Instead, My peace invites believers to lay open their hearts and trust Me.

Shalom,

The Prince of Peace

JOHN 14:27 NIV

Peace I leave with you; my peace I give you. I do not give to you as the world gives. Do not let your hearts be troubled and do not be afraid.

"Live in peace with each other. Do not be proud, but make friends with those who seem unimportant. Do not think how smart you are."

ROMANS 12:16 NCV

The mind set on the flesh is death, but the mind set on the Spirit is life and peace.
ROMANS 8:6 NAS

A harvest of righteousness is sown in peace for those who make peace.
JAMES 3:18 NRSV

When people live so that they please the LORD, even their enemies will make peace with them.
PROVERBS 16:7 NCV

PSALM 34:14 TLB

Turn from all known sin and spend your time in doing good. Try to live in peace with everyone; work hard at it.

All who listen to me will live in peace and safety, unafraid of harm.
PROVERBS 1:33 NLT

In everything, by prayer and petition, with thanksgiving, present your requests to God. And the peace of God, which transcends all understanding, will guard your hearts and your minds in Christ Jesus.
PHILIPPIANS 4:6-7 NIV

Peace

Extreme Protection

Dear Loved One,

If you had any idea of how carefully I watch over you—even sending My angels to protect you—you would be totally amazed! This doesn't mean that you should take your safety for granted or indulge in foolish risks. What it does mean is that your life is really and truly in My hands. I want you to live peacefully, confidently, knowing that I am always there looking after you, in the good times and in the bad.

Release to Me the fears and anxieties that worry and threaten you, and take My hand. Place your trust in Me, and you will never be alone.

In love,

Your Protector

PSALM 121:7-8 NIV

The LORD will keep you from all harm—he will watch over your life; the LORD will watch over your coming and going both now and forevermore.

❝You will have courage because you will have hope. You will take your time, and rest in safety. You will lie down unafraid and many will look to you for help.❞

JOB 11:18-19 TLB

Who is there to harm you if you prove zealous for what is good?
1 PETER 3:13 NAS

He who dwells in the secret place of the Most High shall abide under the shadow of the Almighty. I will say of the LORD, "He is my refuge and my fortress; my God, in Him I will trust."
PSALM 91:1-2 NKJV

HEBREWS 13:6 NIV

We say with confidence, "The Lord is my helper; I will not be afraid. What can man do to me?"

Cast your burden on the LORD, and He shall sustain you; He shall never permit the righteous to be moved.
PSALM 55:22 NKJV

Take up the whole armor of God, so that you may be able to withstand on that evil day, and having done everything, to stand firm.
EPHESIANS 6:13 NRSV

The LORD is my strength and my might; he has become my salvation.
PSALM 118:14 NRSV

Protection

Needs Met

One Whom I Love,

Every day of your life you have needs. There are needs that you barely notice, like the air you breathe and gravity that keeps you safely tethered to the earth. Some of your needs are obvious, and others are seen only by Me. Some of your needs are great, and some are small. I want to meet all of them.

Remember how I take care of the birds by giving them enough food for each day and how I adorn the flowers by clothing them in beautiful colors. Just imagine how much more I desire to care for you! The next time you feel concern over something that is lacking in your life, come to Me. Give Me an opportunity to provide for all your needs!

Abundantly,

Your Provider

2 CORINTHIANS 9:8 NIV

God is able to make all grace abound to you, so that in all things at all times, having all that you need, you will abound in every good work.

> **"Why do you worry about clothing? Consider the lilies of the field, how they grow: they neither toil nor spin; and yet I say to you that even Solomon in all his glory was not arrayed like one of these. Now if God so clothes the grass of the field, which today is, and tomorrow is thrown into the oven, will He not much more clothe you, O you of little faith?"**

MATTHEW 6:28-30 NKJV

PHILIPPIANS 4:19
NIV

My God will meet all your needs according to his glorious riches in Christ Jesus.

He did not leave Himself without witness, in that He did good and gave you rains from heaven and fruitful seasons, satisfying your hearts with food and gladness.
ACTS 14:17 NAS

The LORD will guide you always; he will satisfy your needs in a sun-scorched land and will strengthen your frame. You will be like a well-watered garden, like a spring whose waters never fail.
ISAIAH 58:11 NIV

Dear friend, I am praying that all is well with you and that your body is as healthy as I know your soul is.
3 JOHN 2 TLB

Provision

> **"Though I walk in the midst of trouble, You will revive me; You will stretch out Your hand against the wrath of my enemies, and Your right hand will save me. The LORD will perfect that which concerns me; Your mercy, O LORD, endures forever; do not forsake the works of Your hands."**
>
> PSALM 138:7-8 NKJV

"So therefore, do not be afraid; I will provide for you and your little ones." So he comforted them and spoke kindly to them.
GENESIS 50:21 NAS

Take delight in the LORD, and he will give you the desires of your heart.
PSALM 37:4 NRSV

He satisfies the thirsty and fills up the hungry.
PSALM 107:9 NCV

Jesus replied, "I am the Bread of Life. No one coming to me will ever be hungry again. Those believing in me will never thirst."
JOHN 6:35 TLB

I will lie down in peace and sleep, for you alone, O LORD, will keep me safe.
PSALM 4:8 NLT

Needs Met

> **"Why be like the pagans who are so deeply concerned about these things? Your heavenly Father already knows all your needs."**
>
> MATTHEW 6:32 NLT

I will provide for you there, because five years of famine are still to come. Otherwise you and your household and all who belong to you will become destitute.
GENESIS 45:11 NIV

All mankind scratches for its daily bread, but your heavenly Father knows your needs.
LUKE 12:30 TLB

JOHN 16:23 TLB

At that time you won't need to ask me for anything, for you can go directly to the Father and ask him, and he will give you what you ask for because you use my name.

May He who supplies seed to the sower, and bread for food, supply and multiply the seed you have sown and increase the fruits of your righteousness, while you are enriched in everything for all liberality, which causes thanksgiving through us to God.
2 CORINTHIANS 9:10-11 NKJV

Provision

Seed Faith

Dear Friend,

Do you sometimes feel your faith is way too small—or even that it's hardly there at all? Don't worry. I don't expect you to grow in faith all on your own. I want to help you.

Faith is like a tiny mustard seed. When that little seed is planted in rich, fertile soil, it grows and grows until it becomes a strong and mighty tree. I have instilled in the germ of the seed the power to grow to great proportions despite its tiny beginnings. The same principle is true when you plant a tiny "seed" of faith in the rich, fertile soil of your heart.

It is your job to prepare your heart to receive the seed. Allow Me to "till" the soil with My love and grace. Then be faithful to water the seed with My words of life. Be careful to keep the weeds from crowding out your seed by owning up to your mistakes and asking Me to help you resist temptation. In time, just like that mustard seed, your faith will grow to be strong and healthy!

Faithfully yours,

The Everlasting Father

MATTHEW 17:20 NIV

He replied, "Because you have so little faith. I tell you the truth, if you have faith as small as a mustard seed, you can say to this mountain, 'Move from here to there' and it will move. Nothing will be impossible for you."

40

> **" Faith is the assurance of things hoped for, the conviction of things not seen. "**
>
> HEBREWS 11:1 NAS

When the Holy Spirit controls our lives he will produce this kind of fruit in us: love, joy, peace, patience, kindness, goodness, faithfulness, gentleness and self-control.
GALATIANS 5:22-23 TLB

Those who know Your name will put their trust in You; for You, LORD, have not forsaken those who seek You.
PSALM 9:10 NKJV

MARK 11:22 NIV

"Have faith in God," Jesus answered.

He replied, "If you have faith as small as a mustard seed, you can say to this mulberry tree, 'Be uprooted and planted in the sea,' and it will obey you."
LUKE 17:6 NIV

By continuing to have faith you will save your lives.
LUKE 21:19 NCV

Then Jesus told them, "Truly, if you have faith, and don't doubt, you can do things like this and much more. You can even say to this Mount of Olives, 'Move over into the ocean,' and it will."
MATTHEW 21:21 TLB

Faith

Prayer Line

Dear Friend,

Do you ever feel lonely or long for someone to talk to, someone who will listen and understand? I want you to know that I am a friend who is always there for you, twenty-four hours a day, seven days a week. I am with you in the middle of the night and in the middle of the day.

No matter when you need Me, I'll be there. I don't take off for holidays, and My line is never, ever busy. I am always waiting for you to call out to Me, and I am constantly ready and eager to answer.

Nothing you can tell Me is too shocking or awful. Believe Me, I've heard and seen it all. Besides, I already know everything about you, and I still love you! So please come to Me. Tell Me what's going on in your heart. Let's talk it all over. And don't be surprised if you come away with some very real answers!

Waiting for your call,

Your Loving Father

JOHN 14:14 NCV

If you ask me for anything in my name, I will do it.

> **Ask, and you will be given what you ask for. Seek, and you will find. Knock, and the door will be opened. For everyone who asks, receives. Anyone who seeks, finds. If only you will knock, the door will open.**
>
> MATTHEW 7:7-8 TLB

I say to you, all things for which you pray and ask, believe that you have received them, and they will be granted you.
MARK 11:24 NAS

You shall call, and the Lord will answer; you shall cry, and He will say, "Here I am."
ISAIAH 58:9 NKJV

MATTHEW 6:8 TLB

Remember, your Father knows exactly what you need even before you ask him!

If my people who are called by my name will humble themselves and pray and seek my face and turn from their wicked ways, I will hear from heaven and will forgive their sins and heal their land.
2 CHRONICLES 7:14 NLT

The Lord does not listen to the wicked, but he hears the prayers of those who do right.
PROVERBS 15:29 NCV

Prayer

> **The righteous cry out, and the LORD hears, and delivers them out of all their troubles.**
>
> PSALM 34:17 NKJV

This is the confidence we have in approaching God: that if we ask anything according to his will, he hears us. And if we know that he hears us—whatever we ask—we know that we have what we asked of him.
1 JOHN 5:14-15 NIV

Delight yourself also in the LORD, and He shall give you the desires of your heart.
PSALM 37:4 NKJV

Now about prayer. When you pray, don't be like the hypocrites who love to pray publicly on street corners and in the synagogues where everyone can see them. I assure you, that is all the reward they will ever get. But when you pray, go away by yourself, shut the door behind you, and pray to your Father secretly. Then your Father, who knows all secrets, will reward you.
MATTHEW 6:5-6 NLT

Call to Me, and I will answer you, and show you great and mighty things, which you do not know.
JEREMIAH 33:3 NKJV

> **" Therefore I say to you, whatever things you ask when you pray, believe that you receive them, and you will have them. "**

MARK 11:24 NKJV

Pray to the LORD for the city where you are living, because if good things happen in the city, good things will happen to you also.
JEREMIAH 29:7 NCV

The Spirit helps us in our weakness; for we do not know how to pray as we ought, but that very Spirit intercedes with sighs too deep for words.
ROMANS 8.26 NRSV

1 CORINTHIANS 14:15 NRSV

What should I do then? I will pray with the spirit, but I will pray with the mind also; I will sing praise with the spirit, but I will sing praise with the mind also.

For this reason, all who obey you should pray to you while they still can. When troubles rise like a flood, they will not reach them.
PSALM 32:6 NCV

With God, everything is possible.
MATTHEW 19:26 TLB

We receive from him whatever we ask, because we obey his commandments and do what pleases him.
1 JOHN 3:22 NRSV

Prayer

Hanging Together

My Own Child,

I know how you long for friends you can depend on, people you can laugh or even cry with. I understand how the road can become long and lonely if you have to travel alone. You find strength in numbers and power in unity. I made you that way for a very special purpose. I want you to reach out to others. I want you to be a blessing to others and be blessed by spending time with those I have placed in your life.

I urge you to choose your friends wisely, however. Set your heart on those who know Me and walk in My ways. I know the depth of sharing you can experience with them. I know how you can encourage and help each other along life's road. Together you can reach out to others and show them how much I love you by the example of how you love and care for each other.

Because I care,

The Father of All

ROMANS 12:10 NIV

Be devoted to one another in brotherly love. Honor one another above yourselves.

"Two are better than one, because they have a good reward for their labor. For if they fall, one will lift up his companion. But woe to him who is alone when he falls, for he has no one to help him up. "

ECCLESIASTES 4:9-10 NKJV

Dear friends, let us practice loving each other, for love comes from God and those who are loving and kind show that they are the children of God, and that they are getting to know him better. But if a person isn't loving and kind, it shows that he doesn't know God—for God is love.
1 JOHN 4:7-8 TLB

PSALM 119:63 NIV

I am a friend to all who fear you, to all who follow your precepts.

A new command I give you: Love one another. As I have loved you, so you must love one another. By this all men will know that you are my disciples, if you love one another.
JOHN 13:34-35 NIV

Accept one another, therefore, just as Christ accepted you, for the glory of God.
ROMANS 15:7 MLB

Do nothing out of selfish ambition or vain conceit, but in humility consider others better than yourselves. Each of you should look not only to your own interests, but also to the interests of others.
PHILIPPIANS 2:3-4 NIV

Fellowship

> **A true friend is always loyal, and a brother is born to help in time of need.**
>
> PROVERBS 17:17 TLB

If we live in the light, as God is in the light, we can share fellowship with each other. Then the blood of Jesus, God's Son, cleanses us from every sin.
1 JOHN 1:7 NCV

I am a friend to all who fear you, to all who follow your precepts.
PSALM 119:63 NIV

They were continually devoting themselves to the apostles' teaching and to fellowship, to the breaking of bread and to prayer.
ACTS 2:42 NAS

Do not be unequally yoked together with unbelievers. For what fellowship has righteousness with lawlessness? And what communion has light with darkness?
2 CORINTHIANS 6:14 NKJV

He said to him, "'You shall love the Lord your God with all your heart, and with all your soul, and with all your mind.' This is the greatest and first commandment. And a second is like it: 'You shall love your neighbor as yourself.' On these two commandments hang all the law and the prophets."
MATTHEW 22:37-40 NRSV

> **Do not let loyalty and faithfulness forsake you; bind them around your neck, write them on the tablet of your heart.**
>
> PROVERBS 3:3 NRSV

We proclaim to you what we have seen and heard, so that you also may have fellowship with us. And our fellowship is with the Father and with his Son, Jesus Christ.
1 JOHN 1:3 NIV

They have told the church here of your friendship and your loving deeds. You do well to send them on their way in a manner that pleases God.
3 JOHN 6 NLT

2 SAMUEL 1:26 NCV
I cry for you, my brother Jonathan. I enjoyed your friendship so much. Your love to me was wonderful, better than the love of women.

My loyalty and love will be with him. Through me he will be strong.
PSALM 89:24 NCV

Love must be sincere. Hate what is evil; cling to what is good.
ROMANS 12:9 NIV

Share the joy of those who are happy and the grief of those who grieve.
ROMANS 12:15 MLB

Fellowship

Real Friends

Dear Friend,

Do you know what it means to be a "real" friend? Certainly, there are all kinds of friends in this world, and all are necessary and important in their own way. But during your life you will find that some friends are not as dependable as others. Some will require a lot of love and acceptance, but may not always give it back in return. And that's okay as long as you don't always expect everyone to love you back.

But "real" friends are something special. Very precious because they are so few, these friends will stand by you through all sorts of tough times and always believe the best in you. I urge you to carefully tend to these types of friendships and make yourself as dependable to them as they are to you. These lasting friendships are the ones to be cherished and protected.

All My love,

Your Very Best Friend

I JOHN 4:11 NIV

Dear friends, since God so loved us, we also ought to love one another.

> **Let us consider how we may spur one another on toward love and good deeds. Let us not give up meeting together, as some are in the habit of doing, but let us encourage one another—and all the more as you see the Day approaching.**
>
> HEBREWS 10:24-25 NIV

Now you can have real love for everyone because your souls have been cleansed from selfishness and hatred when you trusted Christ to save you; so see to it that you really do love each other warmly, with all your hearts.
1 PETER 1:22 TLB

JOHN 15:13 NAS

Greater love has no one than this, that one lay down his life for his friends.

A man who has friends must himself be friendly, but there is a friend who sticks closer than a brother.
PROVERBS 18:24 NKJV

A true friend is always loyal, and a brother is born to help in time of need.
PROVERBS 17:17 TLB

Love one another with mutual affection; outdo one another in showing honor.
ROMANS 12:10 NRSV

Friends

> **Some friends may ruin
> you, but a real friend will be
> more loyal than a brother.**
>
> PROVERBS 18:24 NCV

Make no friendship with an angry
man, and with a furious man do
not go.
PROVERBS 22:24 NKJV

Will your love be told in the grave?
Will your loyalty be told in the place
of death?
PSALM 88:11 NCV

Wounds from a friend are better than
many kisses from an enemy.
PROVERBS 27:6 NLT

It is you, a person like me,
my companion and good friend.
We had a good friendship
and walked together to God's Temple.
PSALM 55:13-14 NCV

Rejoice with those who rejoice, and
weep with those who weep.
ROMANS 12:15 NKJV

As iron sharpens iron, so one man
sharpens another.
PROVERBS 27:17 NIV

> **"He who loves a pure heart and whose speech is gracious will have the king for his friend."**
>
> PROVERBS 22:11 NIV

My purpose is that they may be encouraged in heart and united in love, so that they may have the full riches of complete understanding, in order that they may know the mystery of God, namely, Christ.
COLOSSIANS 2:2 NIV

We took sweet counsel together, and walked to the house of God in the throng.
PSALM 55:14 NKJV

PROVERBS 17:9 NCV

Whoever forgives someone's sin makes a friend, but gossiping about the sin breaks up friendships.

Do not forsake your own friend or your father's friend, and do not go to your brother's house in the day of your calamity; better is a neighbor who is near than a brother far away.
PROVERBS 27:10 NAS

May God, who gives this patience and encouragement, help you live in complete harmony with each other—each with the attitude of Christ Jesus toward the other.
ROMANS 15:5 NLT

Friends

Daily Disciplines

My Own,

Discipline may not be your favorite word, but let's examine it in a different light. When I speak of discipline, I am referring to the nurturing of healthy habits that will encourage you to learn and grow. They will also motivate you to get to know Me better.

I urge you to nurture discipline in your life by practicing these simple things: Keep coming to Me with all of your questions and concerns—in fact, keep talking to Me about everything, for that's how our relationship grows stronger. Read and study My Word (the Bible). I don't expect you to read pages and pages every day. To read and understand just one single verse is fantastic! And then, it's important to practice the things you learn from Me in your daily life. I know it's not always easy, but just ask Me, and I will help. I want very much to see you succeed.

All My best,

Your Heavenly Father

COLOSSIANS 3:23 NIV

Whatever you do, work at it with all your heart, as working for the Lord, not for men.

> **"Take pains with these things; be absorbed in them, so that your progress will be evident to all."**

I TIMOTHY 4:15 NAS

You will seek Me and find Me, when you search for Me with all your heart.
JEREMIAH 29:13 NKJV

I don't mean to say I am perfect. I haven't learned all I should even yet, but I keep working toward that day when I will finally be all that Christ saved me for and wants me to be.
PHILIPPIANS 3:12 TLB

REVELATION 3:19 NLT

I am the one who corrects and disciplines everyone I love. Be diligent and turn from your indifference.

You should realize that just as a parent disciplines a child, the LORD your God disciplines you to help you.
DEUTERONOMY 8:5 NLT

They disciplined us for a short time as seemed best to them, but He disciplines us for our good, so that we may share His holiness.
HEBREWS 12:10 NAS

The LORD disciplines those he loves, as a father the son he delights in.
PROVERBS 3:12 NIV

Habits

Telling Others

Dear Friend,

Did you know that I rely on those who have experienced My love to spread the word to others? Perhaps you have felt an urging inside to share with others what you have found, but you don't know how.

There are many ways to show My love to others. But perhaps the most powerful method is through your actions—the way you live your life. You may not realize it, but people are always watching; and when they meet someone whose life is filled with joy and peace, they want to know that person's secret. They watch to see how such a person acts and reacts to the things that are happening around him or her. And they notice how such a person treats others on a daily basis. When they see someone who is loving, gracious, and kind, someone who easily forgives, encourages, and helps others, they witness a glimpse of My true nature. In those moments, I can shine through.

Reaching out,

The Lord of All

MATTHEW 5:16 NKJV

Let your light so shine before men, that they may see your good works and glorify your Father in heaven.

57

> **"You yourselves are my witnesses that I said, 'I am not the Christ,' but, 'I have been sent ahead of Him.'"**
>
> JOHN 3:28 NAS

If a brother or sister is without clothing and in need of daily food, and one of you says to them, "Go in peace, be warmed and be filled," and yet you do not give them what is necessary for their body, what use is that? Even so faith, if it has no works, is dead, being by itself.
JAMES 2:15-17 NAS

MARK 16:15 NRSV

He said to them, "Go into all the world and proclaim the good news to the whole creation."

He told his disciples, "I have been given all authority in heaven and earth. Therefore go and make disciples in all the nations, baptizing them into the name of the Father and of the Son and of the Holy Spirit, and then teach these new disciples to obey all the commands I have given you; and be sure of this—that I am with you always, even to the end of the world."
MATTHEW 28:18-20 TLB

Good News

This Planet

My Own,

I made this world for you. Isn't it absolutely beautiful! Have you seen My majestic mountain peaks? My deserts, vast and barren? Have you stood by My glorious ocean shores and watched as the white-crested waves tumble in, one after the next, without ever ceasing. Amazing, isn't it?

While it's true that one day (and only I know the day) this earth shall pass away, in the meantime, I have appointed people to be My caretakers. That means you, too. I want My children to enjoy and protect this planet I have created for them, to use its resources with care and maintain them for future generations. If My beautiful skies become brown and dirty or My rivers flow with sludge and debris, then I will no longer be glorified as King of creation. People will no longer look at the works of My hands and realize how much I love them. So partner with Me, My friend, and help take care of My planet.

With love,

The Creator of Heaven and Earth

ROMANS 1:20 MLB

From the creation of the world His invisible qualities, such as His eternal power and divine nature, have been made visible and have been understood through His handiwork. So they are without excuse.

3

> **"You alone are the LORD; You have made heaven, the heaven of heavens, with all their host, the earth and everything on it, the seas and all that is in them, and You preserve them all, the host of heaven worships You."**
>
> NEHEMIAH 9:6 NKJV

By him all things were created: things in heaven and on earth, visible and invisible, whether thrones or powers or rulers or authorities; all things were created by him and for him. He is before all things, and in him all things hold together.

COLOSSIANS 1:16-17 NIV

ROMANS 8:19 NAS

The anxious longing of the creation waits eagerly for the revealing of the sons of God.

Be glad; rejoice forever in my creation. Look! I will recreate Jerusalem as a place of happiness, and her people shall be a joy!

ISAIAH 65:18 TLB

This fulfilled the prophecy that said, "I will speak to you in parables. I will explain mysteries hidden since the creation of the world."

MATTHEW 13:35 NLT

Your kingdom is built on what is right and fair. Love and truth are in all you do.

PSALM 89:14 NCV

Nature

Love Me Wholly

Dear Loved One,

Do you know how much I want you to love Me? Completely, with every fiber of your being—just as I love you. Did you think that I wouldn't need your love? Oh, but I do. I created you for that very purpose.

In fact, I have placed within you a desire to respond to the love I have poured out on you. As you get to know Me, I know you will feel that love growing with each day. You will find that loving Me in this way gives you a sense of fulfillment and satisfaction. And it opens wide your heart so more and more of My love can flow back to you.

Try it and see.

All My love,

Your Loving Father

ROMANS 8:28 TLB

We know that all that happens to us is working for our good if we love God and are fitting into his plans.

"We know and rely on the love God has for us. God is love. Whoever lives in love lives in God, and God in him. In this way, love is made complete among us so that we will have confidence on the day of judgment, because in this world we are like him. There is no fear in love. But perfect love drives out fear, because fear has to do with punishment. The one who fears is not made perfect in love. We love because he first loved us."

I JOHN 4:16-19 NIV

JOHN 14:23 NAS

Jesus answered and said to him, "If anyone loves Me, he will keep My word; and My Father will love him, and We will come to him and make Our abode with him."

"The most important one," answered Jesus, "is this: 'Hear, O Israel, the Lord our God, the Lord is one. Love the Lord your God with all your heart and with all your soul and with all your mind and with all your strength.' The second is this: 'Love your neighbor as yourself.' There is no commandment greater than these."
MARK 12:29-31 NIV

Go and celebrate with a feast of choice foods and sweet drinks, and share gifts of food with people who have nothing prepared. This is a sacred day before our Lord. Don't be dejected and sad, for the joy of the LORD is your strength!
NEHEMIAH 8:10 NLT

Surrender

"If we love God, we will do whatever he tells us to. And he has told us from the very first to love each other."

2 JOHN 1:6 TLB

It shall be that if you earnestly obey My commandments which I command you today, to love the LORD your God and serve Him with all your heart and with all your soul, then I will give you the rain for your land in its season, the early rain and the latter rain, that you may gather in your grain, your new wine, and your oil.
DEUTERONOMY 11:13-14 NKJV

Now this is eternal life: that they may know you, the only true God, and Jesus Christ, whom you have sent.
JOHN 17:3 NIV

If anyone loves God, this one is known by Him.
1 CORINTHIANS 8:3 NKJV

> **" Those who do what Christ tells them to will learn to love God more and more. That is the way to know whether or not you are a Christian. "**
>
> 1 JOHN 2:5 TLB

As the Father loved Me, I also have loved you; abide in My love. If you keep My commandments, you will abide in My love, just as I have kept My Father's commandments and abide in His love.
JOHN 15:9-10 NKJV

I love you, O LORD, my strength.
PSALM 18:1 NIV

1 JOHN 5:2 NLT

We know we love God's children if we love God and obey his commandments.

As the deer pants for water, so I long for you, O God. I thirst for God, the living God. Where can I find him to come and stand before him?
PSALM 42:1-2 TLB

My child, give me your heart, and let your eyes observe my ways.
PROVERBS 23:26 NRSV

Those who try to make their life secure will lose it, but those who lose their life will keep it.
LUKE 17:33 NRSV

Surrender

Love Yourself

One Whom I Love,

I've written to you about loving Me and loving others, but I also want to ask you if you love yourself. If your answer is no, I want you to think about this. Consider how much I love you, how dear you are to Me, how I accept you just the way you are. Now if I, Almighty God, can love you so much, shouldn't you be willing to love yourself?

What I want you to do is practice loving yourself. This doesn't mean you have to love (or even like) everything you do. But I want you to learn to love and appreciate who you are and how I made you. You are one of a kind, the workmanship of My own hands. Practice seeing yourself as I see you, and commit to loving yourself just one day at a time.

With utmost love,

Your Creator

I TIMOTHY 6:6 NIV

Godliness with contentment is great gain.

> **Long ago the Lord had said to Israel: I have loved you, O my people, with an everlasting love; with loving-kindness I have drawn you to me.**
>
> JEREMIAH 31:3 TLB

Not that I speak in regard to need, for I have learned in whatever state I am, to be content.
PHILIPPIANS 4:11 NKJV

You should know that your body is a temple for the Holy Spirit who is in you. You have received the Holy Spirit from God. So you do not belong to yourselves.
1 CORINTHIANS 6:19 NCV

JAMES 2:8 NRSV

You do well if you really fulfill the royal law according to the scripture, "You shall love your neighbor as yourself."

Do not seek revenge or bear a grudge against one of your people, but love your neighbor as yourself. I am the LORD.
LEVITICUS 19:18 NIV

HONOR YOUR FATHER AND MOTHER; and YOU SHALL LOVE YOUR NEIGHBOR AS YOURSELF.
MATTHEW 19:19 NAS

Wholly Unique

Love Others

Dear Friend,

You are just beginning to understand how much I love you, and you are also growing in your love for Me. But now, I want you to realize that one of the best ways you can love Me is to love those whom I've placed all around you.

I know some of the people around you may seem quite unlovable. Some may even seem downright despicable. But just as I made you, I made them as well. Perhaps these people are struggling with difficult situations in their lives. Perhaps they are unhappy with themselves and feel they are a "lost cause." They may seem hopeless; but I will never give up on them, and I hope you won't give up on them either.

Remember how I said you are My representative? That's especially true in the "love" department. I really need you to show them My love by giving them yours. But be warned—love is powerful, and it can change things, starting with you!

Unconditionally,

Your Loving Father

JAMES 2:8 NAS

If, however, you are fulfilling the royal law according to the Scripture, "YOU SHALL LOVE YOUR NEIGHBOR AS YOURSELF," you are doing well.

❝Dear friends, let us love one another, for love comes from God. Everyone who loves has been born of God and knows God. Whoever does not love does not know God, because God is love.❞

1 JOHN 4:7-8 NIV

Love is patient, love is kind. It does not envy, it does not boast, it is not proud. It is not rude, it is not self-seeking, it is not easily angered, it keeps no record of wrongs. Love does not delight in evil but rejoices with the truth. It always protects, always trusts, always hopes, always perseveres.

1 CORINTHIANS 13:4-7 NIV

1 JOHN 2:10 TLB

Whoever loves his fellow man is "walking in the light" and can see his way without stumbling around in darkness and sin.

If someone says, "I love God," and hates his brother, he is a liar; for he who does not love his brother whom he has seen, how can he love God whom he has not seen?

1 JOHN 4:20 NKJV

Do not let loyalty and faithfulness forsake you; bind them around your neck, write them on the tablet of your heart.

PROVERBS 3:3 NRSV

Love for Others

I tell you: Love your enemies and
pray for those who persecute you,
that you may be sons of your Father
in heaven. He causes his sun to rise
on the evil and the good, and sends
rain on the righteous and the
unrighteous.
MATTHEW 5:44-45 NIV

I keep hearing of your love and trust
in the Lord Jesus and in his people.
PHILEMON 5 TLB

The second is: "You must love others
as much as yourself." No other
commandments are greater than
these....And I know it is far more
important to love him with all my
heart and understanding and
strength, and to love others as
myself, than to offer all kinds of
sacrifices on the altar of the Temple.
MARK 12:31,33 TLB

Love Others

"Don't just pretend that you love others. Really love them. Hate what is wrong. Stand on the side of the good. "

ROMANS 12:9 NLT

If I had the gift of being able to speak in other languages without learning them, and could speak in every language there is in all of heaven and earth, but didn't love others, I would only be making noise. If I had the gift of prophecy and knew all about what is going to happen in the future, knew everything about everything, but didn't love others, what good would it do? Even if I had the gift of faith so that I could speak to a mountain and make it move, I would still be worth nothing at all without love. If I gave everything I have to poor people, and if I were burned alive for preaching the Gospel but didn't love others, it would be of no value whatever.

1 CORINTHIANS 13:1-3 TLB

Let all that you do be done with love.

1 CORINTHIANS 16:14 NKJV

I THESSALONIANS 3:12 NCV

May the Lord make your love grow more and multiply for each other and for all people so that you will love others as we love you.

Love for Others

Forgive Others

Dear Forgiven One,

You know that I have forgiven you—
completely and totally—for all the
wrongs you have done. Well, that's just
the way I want you to forgive others.

Did you know that I forgave you back at the
Cross before you ever asked? In that same
way, I want you to forgive others even
before they ask. I know that doesn't always
seem fair, but that is the kind of forgiveness
I have given you.

I love you and want only the best for you.
That's why I'm anxious for you to learn to
begin forgiving the moment you realize
you've been wronged. It is the only way for
you to experience true peace. Unforgiveness
quickly turns to bitterness, and where there
is bitterness, there can be no peace. So let
Me help you forgive quickly, and see how
much better you feel.

With grace,

The One Who Laid Down His Life

COLOSSIANS 3:13 TLB

Be gentle and ready to
forgive; never hold
grudges. Remember, the
Lord forgave you, so you
must forgive others.

> **Then Peter came to him and asked, 'Sir, how often should I forgive a brother who sins against me? Seven times?' 'No!' Jesus replied, 'seventy times seven!'**
>
> MATTHEW 18:21-22 TLB

Be kind to one another, tender-hearted, forgiving each other, just as God in Christ also has forgiven you.
EPHESIANS 4:32 NAS

Since you have been chosen by God who has given you this new kind of life, and because of his deep love and concern for you, you should practice tenderhearted mercy and kindness to others. Don't worry about making a good impression on them but be ready to suffer quietly and patiently.
COLOSSIANS 3:12 TLB

I JOHN 1:9 NIV

If we confess our sins, he is faithful and just and will forgive us our sins and purify us from all unrighteousness.

Most important of all, continue to show deep love for each other, for love covers a multitude of sins.
1 PETER 4:8 NLT

Love your enemies! Pray for those who persecute you!
MATTHEW 5:44 TLB

Forgiveness

" If you forgive others for their transgressions, your heavenly Father will also forgive you. But if you do not forgive others, then your Father will not forgive your transgressions. **"**

MATTHEW 6:14-15 NAS

I wrote to you as I did to find out how far you would go in obeying me. When you forgive this man, I forgive him, too. And when I forgive him (for whatever is to be forgiven), I do so with Christ's authority for your benefit, so that Satan will not outsmart us. For we are very familiar with his evil schemes.
2 CORINTHIANS 2:9-11 NLT

In him we have redemption through his blood, the forgiveness of our trespasses, according to the riches of his grace.
EPHESIANS 1:7 NRSV

Now about brotherly love we do not need to write to you, for you yourselves have been taught by God to love each other. And in fact, you do love all the brothers throughout Macedonia. Yet we urge you, brothers, to do so more and more.
1 THESSALONIANS 4:9-10 NIV

Forgive Others

> **Lord, you are kind and forgiving and have great love for those who call to you.**
>
> PSALM 86:5 NCV

What a difference between our sin and God's generous gift of forgiveness. For this one man, Adam, brought death to many through his sin. But this other man, Jesus Christ, brought forgiveness to many through God's bountiful gift.
ROMANS 5:15 NLT

LUKE 17:4 TLB

Even if he wrongs you seven times a day and each time turns again and asks forgiveness, forgive him.

Oh, do not hold us guilty for our former sins! Let your tenderhearted mercies meet our needs, for we are brought low to the dust.
PSALM 79:8 TLB

Do not avenge yourself or bear a grudge against the children of your people, but love your neighbor as yourself. I am the Lord.
LEVITICUS 19:18 MLB

Accept into your group someone who is weak in faith, and do not argue about opinions.
ROMANS 14:1 NCV

Forgiveness

Unless you are Me,
the almighty God, it's
best not to judge others.

Judge Not

One Whom I Love,

People judge others for many reasons. Some are critical because they're unhappy themselves; some put people down because it makes them feel more important; some are simply thoughtless or unkind. This is a dangerous behavior that I hope you will avoid. I, alone, am the righteous judge.

When you are tempted to judge another person, remember that there are many things you may not know. Perhaps that person is struggling with disappointment or heartbreak. Perhaps that person has not yet found peace or happiness. Instead of judging, ask Me to fill you with love and compassion. Ask Me to keep your heart free from sin.

In perfect love,

The Lord Your God

MATTHEW 7:1 NKJV

Judge not, that you be not judged.

> **Let us stop passing judgment on one another. Instead, make up your mind not to put any stumbling block or obstacle in your brother's way.**

ROMANS 14:13 NIV

Only he who made the law can rightly judge among us. He alone decides to save us or destroy. So what right do you have to judge or criticize others?
JAMES 4:12 TLB

Stop judging others, and you will not be judged. Stop criticizing others, or it will all come back on you. If you forgive others, you will be forgiven.
LUKE 6:37 NLT

JOHN 7:24 NKJV

Do not judge according to appearance, but judge with righteous judgment.

Finally, all of you be of one mind, having compassion for one another; love as brothers, be tenderhearted, be courteous; not returning evil for evil or reviling for reviling, but on the contrary blessing, knowing that you were called to this, that you may inherit a blessing.
1 PETER 3:8-9 NKJV

Accepting Others

Handmade by God

Dear Friend,

You sometimes look at yourself and don't like what you see. You think, Oh, if only this or that were different, then I would look so much better. And although I understand your thinking, I happen to know that it's limited to a human perspective.

You do not see the bigger picture, and I don't expect you to. But I do expect you to trust Me—and know that I designed you just as you are for a very specific reason. In My eyes, you're made perfectly, but you're in process. And with Me, you can only improve over time.

So just as I have asked you not to judge others, I also ask you not to judge yourself. Do not question the way I have made you. Trust Me for My workmanship. Believe that, in My hands, you will constantly improve, from the inside out! Try to see yourself as I see you—as My perfectly wonderful creation!

With love,

Your Gracious
and Loving Father

GENESIS 1:27 NKJV

God created man in His own image; in the image of God He created him; male and female He created them.

"You created my inmost being; you knit me together in my mother's womb. I praise you because I am fearfully and wonderfully made; your works are wonderful, I know that full well."

PSALM 139:13-14 NIV

If anyone is in Christ, he is a new creation; the old has gone, the new has come!
2 CORINTHIANS 5:17 NIV

Know that the LORD is God. It is he that made us, and we are his; we are his people, and the sheep of his pasture.
PSALM 100:3 NRSV

I TIMOTHY 4:4 NAS

Everything created by God is good, and nothing is to be rejected, if it is received with gratitude.

You belong to Christ, so you are Abraham's descendants. You will inherit all of God's blessings because of the promise God made to Abraham.
GALATIANS 3:29 NCV

In My Image

> **God created man in His own image, in the image of God He created him; male and female He created them.**
>
> GENESIS 1:27 NAS

From the fruit of his words a man is well satisfied, and the work of a man's hands will come back to him.
PROVERBS 12:14 MLB

Bless the LORD, O my soul; and all that is within me, bless His holy name! Bless the LORD, O my soul, and forget not all His benefits: who forgives all your iniquities, who heals all your diseases, who redeems your life from destruction, who crowns you with lovingkindness and tender mercies, who satisfies your mouth with good things, so that your youth is renewed like the eagle's.
PSALM 103:1-5 NKJV

God's ways are as hard to discern as the pathways of the wind, and as mysterious as a tiny baby being formed in a mother's womb.
ECCLESIASTES 11:5 NLT

God had special plans for me and set me apart for his work even before I was born.
GALATIANS 1:15 NCV

> ❝Thank you for making me so wonderfully complex! It is amazing to think about. Your workmanship is marvelous—and how well I know it.❞
>
> PSALM 139:14 TLB

We are His workmanship, created in Christ Jesus for good works, which God prepared beforehand that we should walk in them.
EPHESIANS 2:10 NKJV

By You I have been sustained from my birth; You are He who took me from my mother's womb; my praise is continually of You.
PSALM 71:6 NAS

ISAIAH 45:12 NAS

It is I who made the earth, and created man upon it. I stretched out the heavens with My hands and I ordained all their host.

Your hands have made and fashioned me; give me understanding that I may learn your commandments.
PSALM 119:73 NRSV

Since you are God's children, God sent the Spirit of his Son into your hearts, and the Spirit cries out, "Father." So now you are not a slave; you are God's child, and God will give you the blessing he promised, because you are his child.
GALATIANS 4:6-7 NCV

In My Image

Our Differences

My One and Only,

There is not, nor has there ever been, anyone just like you! I have made every single person unique and special. How boring it would be if everyone looked the same. I have filled My world with people of many colors, sizes, and styles.

Some people will tell you that you need to conform, to fashion yourself after one group or another. They may urge you to surrender your individuality by wearing the same clothes or fixing your hair the same way. Some might even encourage you to endure painful procedures to mold yourself into what they consider a "perfect" image. But that is not what I intended. Not at all! My way to measure beauty is not the world's way. For I look at your heart.

So rejoice in the differences! Be glad that you're one of a kind. Try to see others through My eyes and beyond the exterior to what lies beneath.

Forever yours,

The Creative Creator

PSALM 17:15 NAS

As for me, I shall behold Your face in righteousness; I will be satisfied with Your likeness when I awake.

❝Be perfect, therefore, as your heavenly Father is perfect.❞

MATTHEW 5:48 NIV

Take a look at the hippopotamus! I made him, too, just as I made you!
JOB 40:15 TLB

Who sees anything different in you? What do you have that you did not receive? And if you received it, why do you boast as if it were not a gift?
1 CORINTHIANS 4:7 NRSV

There are differences of ministries, but the same Lord.
1 CORINTHIANS 12:5 NKJV

1 CORINTHIANS 11:19 NIV

No doubt there have to be differences among you to show which of you have God's approval.

I will be your God throughout your lifetime—until your hair is white with age. I made you, and I will care for you. I will carry you along and save you.
ISAIAH 46:4 NLT

It is better to be humble and be with those who suffer than to share stolen property with the proud.
PROVERBS 16:19 NCV

Self-Acceptance

Life's Not Perfect

Dear Friend,

I cannot promise you a life of perfect ease, free from problems, filled with beauty and bliss. As you know, life's not perfect. It never will be, not on earth anyway.

I can promise My guidance along the way, My strength to carry you through tough times, and My presence to comfort you through your sorrows. I invite you to give all your expectations to Me. Trust Me with your future. Believe that I have good things, yes even wonderful things, in store for you. Certainly there will be many times when life may actually seem quite perfect, but keep in mind that My definition of perfection differs from yours.

Remember, life on this earth will never be perfect. But as you pass through life's trials and challenges, I will be with you, and I will give you "perfect" peace.

Trust Me,

Your Faithful Father

MARK 11:22 NIV

"Have faith in God," Jesus answered.

"Cast your burden on the LORD, and He shall sustain you; He shall never permit the righteous to be moved."

PSALM 55:22 NKJV

So be truly glad! There is wonderful joy ahead, even though the going is rough for a while down here. These trials are only to test your faith, to see whether or not it is strong and pure. It is being tested as fire tests gold and purifies it—and your faith is far more precious to God than mere gold; so if your faith remains strong after being tried in the test tube of fiery trials, it will bring you much praise and glory and honor on the day of his return. You love him even though you have never seen him; though not seeing him, you trust him; and even now you are happy with the inexpressible joy that comes from heaven itself.

1 PETER 1:6-8 TLB

NUMBERS 23:19 NKJV

God is not a man, that He should lie, nor a son of man, that He should repent. Has He said, and will He not do? Or has He spoken, and will He not make it good?

When you pass through the waters, I will be with you; and through the rivers, they shall not overflow you. When you walk through the fire, you shall not be burned, nor shall the flame scorch you.

ISAIAH 43:2 NKJV

Disappointment

True Perfection

Dear Friend,

I have instilled in all human beings a deep desire to seek out what is pure and holy and right. You may at times get sidetracked with life's many distractions, but that longing is always present deep down inside you.

This inner longing will draw you to the Light, to all things that are good and perfect and true. It will draw you to Me, because I am the Light of the World. Listen to your heart, and it will cause you to seek Me—the same way someone lost in the darkness gravitates toward the light or someone who is cold draws close to the fire for warmth.

The light of My love casts no shadows. It will not disappoint or confuse. It provides direction and confidence as you pass through difficulties and climb over obstacles. Listen to your heart. It will show you the way.

In perfect and everlasting love,

Your Holy God

2 CORINTHIANS 7:1 NIV

Since we have these promises, dear friends, let us purify ourselves from everything that contaminates body and spirit, perfecting holiness out of reverence for God.

"When Jesus spoke again to the people, he said, 'I am the light of the world. Whoever follows me will never walk in darkness, but will have the light of life.'"

JOHN 8:12 NIV

They cried to You, and were delivered; they trusted in You, and were not ashamed.
PSALM 22:5 NKJV

God's laws are perfect. They protect us, make us wise, and give us joy and light.
PSALM 19:7-8 TLB

EPHESIANS 1:3 NKJV

As for God, His way is perfect; the word of the LORD is proven; He is a shield to all who trust in Him.
PSALM 18:30 NKJV

Blessed be the God and Father of our Lord Jesus Christ, who has blessed us with every spiritual blessing in the heavenly places in Christ.

Let endurance have its perfect result, so that you may be perfect and complete, lacking in nothing.
JAMES 1:4 NAS

When we have been made perfect and complete, then the need for these inadequate special gifts will come to an end, and they will disappear.
1 CORINTHIANS 13:10 TLB

God's Ways

Time to Trust

My Own,

There are those who have broken your trust. Perhaps not so much because they wanted to hurt you, but merely because they are human. Maybe you've even told yourself that you will never trust anyone again.

But know this: You can trust Me.

You can place your entire heart—your hopes, dreams, desires, expectations, emotions, innermost thoughts—into My hands. You will always, always be safe there. Even now, I invite you to imagine placing your heart in My hands. Maybe you are hurting; perhaps your heart is broken. I am called the Great Physician. It is My delight to touch and heal you. Trust Me with your heart and with every other concern in your life. I will never disappoint you.

Trust Me,

Your Heavenly Father

PSALM 118:8 NAS

It is better to take
refuge in the LORD
Than to trust in man.

"God is our refuge and strength,
an ever-present help in trouble.
Therefore we will not fear,
though the earth give way
and the mountains fall
into the heart of the sea."

PSALM 46:1-2 NIV

Humble yourselves under the
mighty hand of God, that He may
exalt you in due time, casting all
your care upon Him,
for He cares for you.
1 PETER 5:6-7 NKJV

This is the boldness we have in
God's presence: that if we ask God
for anything that agrees with what
he wants, he hears us.
1 JOHN 5:14 NCV

We can say with confidence, "The
Lord is my helper, so I will not be
afraid. What can mere
mortals do to me?"
HEBREWS 13:6 NLT

If you can believe, all things are
possible to him who believes.
MARK 9:23 NKJV

PSALM 40:4 NLT

Oh, the joys of
those who trust
the LORD, who
have no
confidence in
the proud, or in
those who
worship idols.

My Promise

> **" Those who know the LORD
> trust him, because he will not
> leave those who come to him. "**
>
> PSALM 9:10 NCV

Truly, in our own hearts we believed
we would die. But this happened so
we would not trust in ourselves but in
God, who raises people from the dead.
2 CORINTHIANS 1:9 NCV

Through Christ you have come to
trust in God. And because God raised
Christ from the dead and gave him
great glory, your faith and hope can
be placed confidently in God.
1 PETER 1:21 NLT

Do not let your hearts be troubled.
Believe in God, believe also in me.
JOHN 14:1 NRSV

For this reason I also suffer these
things; nevertheless I am not
ashamed, for I know whom I have
believed and am persuaded that He is
able to keep what I have committed
to Him until that Day.
2 TIMOTHY 1:12 NKJV

> **If you want favor with both God and man, and a reputation for good judgment and common sense, then trust the Lord completely; don't ever trust yourself.**

PROVERBS 3:4-5 TLB

May the God of hope fill you with all joy and peace as you trust in him, so that you may overflow with hope by the power of the Holy Spirit.
ROMANS 15:13 NIV

By awesome deeds You answer us in righteousness, O God of our salvation, You who are the trust of all the ends of the earth and of the farthest sea.
PSALM 65:5 NAS

PSALM 4:5 TLB

Put your trust in the Lord, and offer him pleasing sacrifices.

Because of Christ and our faith in him, we can now come fearlessly into God's presence, assured of his glad welcome.
EPHESIANS 3:12 NLT

As the Scripture says, "Anyone who trusts in him will never be disappointed."
ROMANS 10:11 NCV

My Promise

Well of Joy

The source of true joy is found in Me.

My Friend,

Everyone wants to experience joy—the happiness that comes with fun and celebration and laughter. But true joy, that satisfying kind of joy that flows like the purest water bubbling up from the deepest well, is found only in Me.

I invite you to come directly to Me and allow Me to share My joy with you. My joy is hard to describe in earthly words, but it is real and solid and glorious. It is a joy that doesn't depend upon pleasant circumstances but can survive despite the trials of the day. It is a joy that strengthens your spirit and reminds your heart that I, the Lord, am God.

This type of joy only comes as a result of your relationship with Me, but I promise that if you choose to walk with Me, My joy will be a constant part of your life.

Joyfully,

The Lord God Almighty

JOHN 15:11 NKJV

These things I have spoken to you, that My joy may remain in you, and that your joy may be full.

90

"Consider it all joy, my brethren, when you encounter various trials, knowing that the testing of your faith produces endurance."

JAMES 1:2-3 NAS

May the godly man exult. May he rejoice and be merry.
PSALM 68:3 TLB

When I remember these things, I pour out my soul within me. For I used to go with the multitude; I went with them to the house of God, with the voice of joy and praise, with a multitude that kept a pilgrim feast.
PSALM 42:4 NKJV

PHILIPPIANS 2:17-18 NAS

Even if I am being poured out as a drink offering upon the sacrifice and service of your faith, I rejoice and share my joy with you all. You too, I urge you, rejoice in the same way and share your joy with me.

He crowns it all with green, lush pastures in the wilderness; hillsides blossom with joy. The pastures are filled with flocks of sheep, and the valleys are carpeted with grain. All the world shouts with joy, and sings.
PSALM 65:11-13 TLB

How great is your goodness that you have stored up for those who fear you, that you have given to those who trust you. You do this for all to see.
PSALM 31:19 NCV

Joy

> **"Shout joyfully to the LORD, all the earth; break forth and sing for joy and sing praises."**
>
> PSALM 98:4 NAS

Well of Joy

Let your roots grow down into him
and draw up nourishment from him.
See that you go on growing in the
Lord, and become strong and vigorous
in the truth you were taught.
Let your lives overflow with joy and
thanksgiving for all he has done.
COLOSSIANS 2:7 TLB

From this we know that we remain in
Him and He in us, because He has
imparted His Spirit to us.
1 JOHN 4:13 MLB

Moses built an altar there and called
it "The LORD Is My Banner."
EXODUS 17:15 NLT

My heart rejoices in the LORD;
in the LORD my horn is lifted high.
My mouth boasts over my enemies,
for I delight in your deliverance.
1 SAMUEL 2:1 NIV

The LORD lives!
May my Rock be praised.
Praise the God who saves me!
PSALM 18:46 NCV

"The Kingdom of God is not a matter of what we eat or drink, but of living a life of goodness and peace and joy in the Holy Spirit."

ROMANS 14:17 NLT

Let all who take refuge in you rejoice; let them sing joyful praises forever. Protect them, so all who love your name may be filled with joy.
PSALM 5:11 NLT

Rejoice in the Lord always. I will say it again: Rejoice!
PHILIPPIANS 4:4 NIV

PSALM 149:5 NAS

Let the godly ones exult in glory; let them sing for joy on their beds.

Always be joyful. Always keep on praying. No matter what happens, always be thankful, for this is God's will for you who belong to Christ Jesus.
1 THESSALONIANS 5:16-18 TLB

Happy are the people who know how to praise you. LORD, let them live in the light of your presence. In your name they rejoice and continually praise your goodness.
PSALM 89:15-16 NCV

Joy

Promoting Peace

Dear Friend,

Everyone is talking about peace these days.
It warms My heart to see people working
together to promote peace, for I find no
delight in war and killing.

Unfortunately, world peace will never be a
complete reality until the day when My
peace reigns over the earth. In the
meantime, I urge you to practice and
promote peace in your own corner of the
world. Be a peacemaker in your home, your
school, your community.

And here's the secret to being a
peacemaker: Love those around you—
your family, your friends, your neighbors,
even your enemies. You may think that
sounds too difficult, even impossible. But
don't forget all things are possible with Me.
And I am more than willing to help you.

Peacefully,

The Lord Your God

MATTHEW 5:9 NIV

Blessed are the
peacemakers, for they
will be called sons of
God.

> **I am leaving you with a gift—peace of mind and heart! And the peace I give isn't fragile like the peace the world gives. So don't be troubled or afraid.**
>
> JOHN 14:27 TLB

The fruit of righteousness is sown in peace by those who make peace.
JAMES 3:18 NKJV

I say to you, love your enemies and pray for those who persecute you.
MATTHEW 5:44 NAS

EPHESIANS 2:14 NIV

He himself is our peace, who has made the two one and has destroyed the barrier, the dividing wall of hostility.

If you do this you will experience God's peace, which is far more wonderful than the human mind can understand. His peace will keep your thoughts and your hearts quiet and at rest as you trust in Christ Jesus.
PHILIPPIANS 4:7 TLB

Since we have been made right with God by our faith, we have peace with God. This happened through our Lord Jesus Christ, who has brought us into that blessing of God's grace that we now enjoy. And we are happy because of the hope we have of sharing God's glory.
ROMANS 5:1-2 NCV

Peacemaker

> **"Keep putting into practice all you learned from me and saw me doing, and the God of peace will be with you."**
>
> PHILIPPIANS 4:9 TLB

Promoting Peace

He himself is our peace, who has made the two one and has destroyed the barrier, the dividing wall of hostility.
EPHESIANS 2:14 NIV

Let the peace of Christ rule in your hearts, to which indeed you were called in one body; and be thankful.
COLOSSIANS 3:15 NAS

The LORD will give strength to His people; the LORD will bless His people with peace.
PSALM 29:11 NKJV

The LORD bless you and keep you; the LORD make his face shine upon you and be gracious to you; the LORD turn his face toward you and give you peace.
NUMBERS 6:24-26 NIV

You will keep him in perfect peace, whose mind is stayed on You, because he trusts in You.
ISAIAH 26:3 NKJV

> **Those who love Your law have great peace, and nothing causes them to stumble.**
>
> PSALM 119:165 NAS

We pursue the things which make for peace and the building up of one another.
ROMANS 14:19 NAS

Do your part to live in peace with everyone, as much as possible.
ROMANS 12:18 NLT

God is not a God of disorder but of peace.
1 CORINTHIANS 14:33 NIV

2 CORINTHIANS
13:11 NKJV

Finally, brethren, farewell. Become complete. Be of good comfort, be of one mind, live in peace; and the God of love and peace will be with you.

The time will come when I will heal Jerusalem's damage and give her prosperity and peace.
JEREMIAH 33:6 TLB

May the Lord of peace Himself grant you peace at all times under all circumstances. The Lord be with you all.
2 THESSALONIANS 3:16 MLB

I say to you, love your enemies and pray for those who persecute you.
MATTHEW 5:44 NAS

Peacemaker

Patiently Waiting

Dear Waiting One,

If you are like most people, you probably don't like to wait. Many people ask Me repeatedly for certain things and impatiently demand instant answers. But when My answer is "no" or "wait," they sometimes grow impatient, even sulk and assume I haven't answered at all.

But just as earthly parents must sometimes give unpopular answers, so must I, your Heavenly Father. And I know it's difficult to wait. But it's during this time that you can best develop patience.

And patience is important, for My timing is definitely not always your timing. But believe Me, My timing is best. It is perfect. If I decide it's better to wait, be assured that I have good reason. I'm looking out for you. I am always seeking your best interest. So the next time I ask you to wait, please, trust Me and practice patience.

My timing is perfect,

The Creator of Time

ROMANS 8:25 NIV

If we hope for what we do not yet have, we wait for it patiently.

> **Yet the LORD longs to be gracious to you; he rises to show you compassion. For the LORD is a God of justice. Blessed are all who wait for him!**
>
> ISAIAH 30:18 NIV

I waited patiently for God to help me;
then he listened and heard my cry.
He lifted me out of the pit of despair,
out from the bog and the mire, and
set my feet on a hard, firm path and
steadied me as I walked along.

PSALM 40:1-2 TLB

ECCLESIASTES 7:8
TLB

Finishing is
better than
starting!
Patience is
better than
pride!

The grace of God that brings
salvation has appeared to all men,
teaching us that, denying
ungodliness and worldly lusts, we
should live soberly, righteously, and
godly in the present age, looking for
the blessed hope and glorious
appearing of our great God and
Savior Jesus Christ.

TITUS 2:11-13 NKJV

Commit your works to the LORD,
and your thoughts will
be established.

PROVERBS 16:3 NKJV

Timing

> **" Patience is better than strength. Controlling your temper is better than capturing a city. "**
>
> PROVERBS 16:32 NCV

Whatever things were written before were written for our learning, that we through the patience and comfort of the Scriptures might have hope. Now may the God of patience and comfort grant you to be like-minded toward one another, according to Christ Jesus.
ROMANS 15:4-5 NKJV

With patience a ruler may be persuaded, and a soft tongue can break bones.
PROVERBS 25:15 NRSV

There is a time for everything, a season for every activity under heaven.
ECCLESIASTES 3:1 NLT

Brothers and sisters, do not be weary in doing what is right.
2 THESSALONIANS 3:13 NRSV

God is at work within you, helping you want to obey him, and then helping you do what he wants.
PHILIPPIANS 2:13 TLB

> **A man's wisdom gives him patience; it is to his glory to overlook an offense.**
>
> PROVERBS 19:11 NIV

We have proved ourselves by our purity, our understanding, our patience, our kindness, our sincere love, and the power of the Holy Spirit.
2 CORINTHIANS 6:6 NLT

You, O man of God, flee these things and pursue righteousness, godliness, faith, love, patience, gentleness.
1 TIMOTHY 6:11 NKJV

HEBREWS 6:12 NAS

That you will not be sluggish, but imitators of those who through faith and patience inherit the promises.

May you be made strong with all the strength that comes from his glorious power, and may you be prepared to endure everything with patience, while joyfully giving thanks to the Father.
COLOSSIANS 1:11-12 NRSV

We must not become tired of doing good. We will receive our harvest of eternal life at the right time if we do not give up.
GALATIANS 6:9 NCV

Timing

Generous Living

Dear Friend,

Do you know how much I love to give good gifts to all My children? Can you imagine how much I delight in creating a glorious sunset full of vibrant shades of red, purple, and pink just to watch as awestruck observers witness this brief moment of splendor?

That, My friend, is the hidden pleasure of generosity. The blessing comes not so much in the receiving as it does in the giving. And you need to know that it's even better when the giving is done in secret. I experience great joy when My children give generously without advertising the fact. And how I love to reward them for it!

What would any of you have if it were not for Me? Isn't everything on earth a gift from your Father above? I encourage you now: Share the abundance of what I have given. And then see if you're not blessed beyond expectation when you give to others. Here's another important tip: When you give, make sure it's from your heart and done with a cheerful spirit. That's the very best way!

Generously yours,

The Giver of Every Good and Perfect Gift

MATTHEW 10:8 TLB

Give as freely as you have received!

> " Give, and it will be given to
> you.... For with the same
> measure that you use, it
> will be measured back to you. "

LUKE 6:38 NKJV

In everything I did, I showed you
that by this kind of hard work we
must help the weak, remembering
the words the Lord Jesus himself
said: "It is more blessed to
give than to receive."
ACTS 20:35 NIV

PROVERBS 18:16
NAS

A man's gift
makes room for
him, and brings
him before
great men.

If you are a preacher, see to it that
your sermons are strong and
helpful. If God has given you money,
be generous in helping others
with it. If God has given you
administrative ability and put you in
charge of the work of others, take
the responsibility seriously. Those
who offer comfort to the sorrowing
should do so with Christian cheer.
ROMANS 12:8 TLB

Whenever you are able, do good
to people who need help.
PROVERBS 3:27 NCV

Good
Gifts

Generous Living

> **It is possible to give away and become richer! It is also possible to hold on too tightly and lose everything. Yes, the liberal man shall be rich! By watering others, he waters himself.**

PROVERBS 11:24-25 TLB

Whatever you do, work at it with all your heart, as working for the Lord, not for men, since you know that you will receive an inheritance from the Lord as a reward. It is the Lord Christ you are serving.
COLOSSIANS 3:23-24 NIV

You are generous because of your faith. And I am praying that you will really put your generosity to work, for in so doing you will come to an understanding of all the good things we can do for Christ.
PHILEMON 6 NLT

Like good stewards of the manifold grace of God, serve one another with whatever gift each of you has received.
1 PETER 4:10 NRSV

You shall surely give to him, and your heart should not be grieved when you give to him, because for this thing the LORD your God will bless you in all your works and in all to which you put your hand.
DEUTERONOMY 15:10 NKJV

❝It is good to be merciful and generous. Those who are fair in their business will never be defeated. ❞

PSALM 112:5 NCV

Take care that you do not despise one of these little ones; for, I tell you, in heaven their angels continually see the face of my Father in heaven.
MATTHEW 18:10 NRSV

He will take care of the helpless and poor when they cry to him; for they have no one else to defend them.
PSALM 72:12 TLB

PROVERBS 22:9 NLT

Blessed are those who are generous, because they feed the poor.

Contributing to the needs of the saints, practicing hospitality.
ROMANS 12:13 MLB

Do not forget to do good and to share with others, for with such sacrifices God is pleased.
HEBREWS 13:16 NIV

Learn to do good, to be fair and to help the poor, the fatherless, and widows.
ISAIAH 1:17 TLB

Good Gifts

Cling to Me and you will have something to show for it.

Bearing Fruit

My Own,

As you grow physically from child to adult, you naturally begin to look different, and your personality and outlook on life also change. Spiritual growth is similar. If you're growing in Me, character traits like love, joy, peace, patience, gentleness, and self-control will appear in your life. Sometimes they even sneak up without your noticing. Some call this type of development "spiritual fruit."

This "fruit" is a natural result of a relationship with Me. In fact, you could compare Me to a fruit tree. I am like the main portion (the trunk and the roots), and those who follow Me are the branches that grow from Me. As long as My branch remains firmly connected to My trunk, it is inevitable that it will bear blossoms, followed by delicious fruit. The stronger and healthier the branch grows, the more fruit it can support.

So connect yourself to Me, and together we will rejoice as all sorts of good fruit begins to appear in your life!

Like a tree,

Your Everlasting Father

2 PETER 1:8 NKJV

If these things are yours and abound, you will be neither barren nor unfruitful in the knowledge of our Lord Jesus Christ.

> **I am the true vine, and my Father is the gardener. He cuts off every branch in me that bears no fruit, while every branch that does bear fruit he prunes so that it will be even more fruitful. You are already clean because of the word I have spoken to you. Remain in me, and I will remain in you. No branch can bear fruit by itself; it must remain in the vine. Neither can you bear fruit unless you remain in me.**

JOHN 15:1-4 NIV

PSALM 1:3 TLB

They are like trees along a river bank bearing luscious fruit each season without fail. Their leaves shall never wither, and all they do shall prosper.

He gives power to those who are tired and worn out; he offers strength to the weak. Even youths will become exhausted, and young men will give up. But those who wait on the LORD will find new strength. They will fly high on wings like eagles. They will run and not grow weary. They will walk and not faint.

ISAIAH 40:29-31 NLT

Spiritual Growth

Helping Others

My Dear Friend,

No one is an island in this world. Whether you are an introvert or an extravert, you touch the lives of many people every day. And all of those people have needs. As you grow stronger in My love and care, I urge you to reach out to them with the same message of hope that you have received. You may feel overwhelmed by this idea, but don't worry. I don't expect you to solve all their problems or even speak to them on your own. All I ask is that you have a tender and willing heart.

The way to help others often begins with prayer. When you come to Me, I can guide you toward those who are open to My touch. And you can pray specifically for them; I will show you how. And I will show you ways to reach out to them with a smile, a hello, or a simple act of kindness. As you become better acquainted with them, they may even grow more open to hearing about Me and how much I love them. Don't be in a big hurry; these things take time. But it's well worth the effort when you reach out and help others.

Your partner,

The Loving Father of All

I JOHN 3:18 NIV

Dear children, let us not love with words or tongue but with actions and in truth.

> **" In everything set them an example by doing what is good. In your teaching show integrity, seriousness and soundness of speech that cannot be condemned, so that those who oppose you may be ashamed because they have nothing bad to say about us. "**
>
> TITUS 2:7-8 NIV

Then the King will say . . . "For I was hungry and you gave Me food; I was thirsty and you gave Me drink; I was a stranger and you took Me in; I was naked and you clothed Me; I was sick and you visited Me; I was in prison and you came to Me." Then the righteous will answer Him saying, "Lord, when did we see You hungry and feed You, or thirsty and give You drink? When did we see You a stranger and take You in, or naked and clothe You? Or when did we see You sick, or in prison, and come to You?" And the King will answer and say to them, "Assuredly, I say to you, inasmuch as you did it to one of the least of these My brethren, you did it to Me."

MATTHEW 25:34-40 NKJV

2 CORINTHIANS 1:12 NAS

Our proud confidence is this: the testimony of our conscience, that in holiness and godly sincerity, not in fleshly wisdom but in the grace of God, we have conducted ourselves in the world, and especially toward you.

Kindness

Beat the Blues

My Own,

I know how you can get discouraged sometimes. It is part of the human condition, and it seems to happen more frequently to people who are tenderhearted. You feel things more deeply, and you take them directly to heart. This can make you "blue."

That's exactly why you need to come to Me when you feel down. Bring Me all your hurts. Bring Me all your disappointments. Come and place all your sadness right into My hands. Allow Me to carry your burdens for you. I am strong and able to bear the toughest loads.

Sadness is a strange thing—the more you hold on to it and keep it to yourself, the larger and more burdensome it will grow.

Bring everything to Me, My child. Leave it all in My hands. As you do, I will fill you once again with My joy.

In gentle love,

Your Comforter

MATTHEW 11:28 NAS

Come to Me, all who are weary and heavy-laden, and I will give you rest.

> **He heals the brokenhearted,
> binding up their wounds.**
>
> PSALM 147:3 TLB

Praise be to the God and Father of
our Lord Jesus Christ, the Father of
compassion and the God of all
comfort, who comforts us in all our
troubles, so that we can comfort
those in any trouble with the
comfort we ourselves have received
from God.
2 CORINTHIANS 1:3-4 NIV

My flesh and my heart fail; but God
is the strength of my heart and
my portion forever.
PSALM 73:26 NKJV

2 CORINTHIANS
7:10 NCV

The kind of
sorrow God
wants makes
people change
their hearts and
lives. This leads
to salvation, and
you cannot be
sorry for that.
But the kind of
sorrow the
world has brings
death.

He turned my sorrow into joy! He
took away my clothes of mourning
and gave me gay and festive
garments to rejoice in.
PSALM 30:11 TLB

His anger lasts for a moment, but
his favor lasts a lifetime! Weeping
may go on all night, but joy comes
with the morning.
PSALM 30:5 NLT

Unburdened

The Next World

One Whom I Love,

Do you sometimes look up at the sky and wonder what Heaven is like? Most of My children do this occasionally. I smile to Myself as I observe the intrigue and fascination on their faces as they try to figure out one of life's greatest unsolved mysteries.

But like an earthly father who is planning a huge surprise birthday party for his much-loved child, I choose to keep most of the glorious details of this upcoming event to Myself. Why spoil the surprise? Part of My delight in creating something as incredibly wonderful as Heaven is witnessing My children's totally amazed faces as they arrive and see it all for the first time. Oh, what a day that will be!

Heaven is absolutely spectacular! If you took every splendid element of earth—things like the Grand Canyon, the depths of the sea, Walt Disney World—and multiplied their glory a million times over, you would not even scratch the surface of Heaven. It defies human imagination. I'll tell you this: The greatest moment will be when you look right into My eyes and see firsthand My never-ending love for you!

In great expectation,

The Creator of
Heaven and Earth

2 CORINTHIANS 5:1 NKJV

We know that if our earthly house, this tent, is destroyed, we have a building from God, a house not made with hands, eternal in the heavens.

❝He will wipe away all tears from their eyes, and there shall be no more death, nor sorrow, nor crying, nor pain. All of that has gone forever.❞

REVELATION 21:4 TLB

Never again will they hunger; never again will they thirst. The sun will not beat upon them, nor any scorching heat. For the Lamb at the center of the throne will be their shepherd; he will lead them to springs of living water. And God will wipe away every tear from their eyes.
REVELATION 7:16-17 NIV

1 JOHN 3:3 TLB

Everyone who really believes this will try to stay pure because Christ is pure.

God blesses those whose hearts are pure, for they will see God.
MATTHEW 5:8 NLT

Night shall be no more; they will need neither lamplight nor sunlight, for the Lord God will be their light, and they shall reign forever and ever.
REVELATION 22:5 MLB

The grace of the Lord Jesus be with all.
REVELATION 22:21 NCV

Heaven

The Next World

> ❝In My Father's house are many dwelling places; if it were not so, I would have told you; for I go to prepare a place for you. If I go and prepare a place for you, I will come again and receive you to Myself, that where I am, there you may be also.❞

JOHN 14:2-3 NAS

I saw a new heaven and a new earth; for the first heaven and the first earth had passed away, and the sea was no more. And I saw the holy city, the new Jerusalem, coming down out of heaven from God, prepared as a bride adorned for her husband.
REVELATION 21:1-2 NRSV

Then we who are alive and remain shall be caught up together with them in the clouds to meet the Lord in the air. And thus we shall always be with the Lord.
1 THESSALONIANS 4:17 NKJV

Now God's presence is with people, and he will live with them, and they will be his people. God himself will be with them and will be their God.
REVELATION 21:3 NCV

> ❝ Let them praise the name of the LORD, For His name alone is exalted; His glory is above the earth and heaven. ❞

PSALM 148:13 NKJV

MATTHEW 5:12
NRSV

Rejoice and be glad, for your reward is great in heaven, for in the same way they persecuted the prophets who were before you.

Listen, I tell you a mystery: We will not all sleep, but we will all be changed—in a flash, in the twinkling of an eye, at the last trumpet. For the trumpet will sound, the dead will be raised imperishable, and we will be changed. For the perishable must clothe itself with the imperishable, and the mortal with immortality. When the perishable has been clothed with the imperishable, and the mortal with immortality, then the saying that is written will come true: "Death has been swallowed up in victory."
1 CORINTHIANS 15:51-54 NIV

They were finally told that these things would not occur during their lifetime, but long years later, during yours. And now at last this Good News has been plainly announced to all of us. It was preached to us in the power of the same heaven-sent Holy Spirit who spoke to them; and it is all so strange and wonderful that even the angels in heaven would give a great deal to know more about it.
1 PETER 1:12 TLB

Heaven

Healed Hearts

My Own Child,

I've been watching over you since before you were born. I know all you've seen and everything you've experienced from your earliest days. I have felt every single hurt you've endured and each tear that you've cried. I know about the inner wounds you bear, and, yes, I can see each scar.

Nothing is hidden from Me, and nothing is too difficult for Me. I long to touch those deep places inside you that still ache and sting. I want to make you healthy and whole. Won't you allow Me to do my healing work in your heart?

As I heal you, I will replace your broken spirit with the wholeness of My spirit. Sometimes healing can take time, but I am all you need. And when I'm finished, you will have a completely new heart, strong enough to hold all the love I have for you.

In gentle love,

The Great Physician

PSALM 147:3 NKJV

He heals the brokenhearted and binds up their wounds.

"Fear not, for I am with you; be not dismayed, for I am your God. I will strengthen you, yes, I will help you, I will uphold you with My righteous right hand. "

ISAIAH 41:10 NKJV

Cast all your anxiety on him because he cares for you.
1 PETER 5:7 NIV

Don't be impatient. Wait for the Lord, and he will come and save you! Be brave, stouthearted and courageous. Yes, wait and he will help you.
PSALM 27:14 TLB

PSALM 34:18 NIV

The LORD is close to the brokenhearted and saves those who are crushed in spirit.

I have told you these things, so that in me you may have peace. In this world you will have trouble. But take heart! I have overcome the world.
JOHN 16:33 NIV

You are a hiding place for me; you preserve me from trouble; you surround me with glad cries of deliverance.
PSALM 32:7 NRSV

Inner Healing

Troubled Hearts

Dear Friend,

Many things that happen on earth are sad and painful. I see those things and feel them deeply. Death and loss, for example, can leave you with confusing emotions and a troubled soul. You should remember, though, that these emotions are normal. They are part of human grief. Even My own Son, Jesus, wept openly when His dear friend Lazarus died suddenly.

You will undoubtedly experience strong emotions like anger, bitterness, and even apathy. You may feel tempted to blame Me for your circumstances. That's okay. All I ask is that you bring those feelings to Me. Come and talk about your anger, your hurt. Though I warn you, some things cannot be fully understood here on earth, I'm confident that we can sort it all out.

Best of all, I can comfort you, My friend. I long to wrap My arms around you, to hold you securely in My love. Come to Me with your hurting heart, and don't be afraid to be honest. I can take it.

With open arms,

The Comforter

PSALM 116:8 NKJV

You have delivered my soul from death, my eyes from tears, and my feet from falling.

> **Even though I walk through the valley of the shadow of death, I will fear no evil, for you are with me; your rod and your staff, they comfort me.**
>
> PSALM 23:4 NIV

PSALM 138:7 NKJV

Though I walk in the midst of trouble, You will revive me; You will stretch out Your hand against the wrath of my enemies, and Your right hand will save me.

I am convinced that nothing can ever separate us from his love. Death can't, and life can't. The angels won't, and all the powers of hell itself cannot keep God's love away. Our fears for today, our worries about tomorrow, or where we are—high above the sky, or in the deepest ocean—nothing will ever be able to separate us from the love of God demonstrated by our Lord Jesus Christ when he died for us.
ROMANS 8:38-39 TLB

The LORD is good,
a stronghold in a day of trouble;
he protects those who take
refuge in him.
NAHUM 1:7 NRSV

When I suffer, this comforts me:
Your promise gives me life.
PSALM 119:50 NCV

Comfort

Hope is found in Me.

Hope in God

My Own,

Hopelessness abounds in the world today. I can see the emptiness of men's hearts even from where I sit, and it grieves Me.

The answer to hopelessness is so simple, so readily available; yet so many close their eyes and miss it completely. Hope is found in Me—real hope, lasting hope, eternal hope. You see, I have a plan for every life, a plan filled with victory and joy and peace.

So when you begin to feel your hope ebbing away, eroded by the fear that life has no purpose and offers you no future, come to Me. Come quickly, and let Me share My hope with you, a hope filled with life and love and fulfillment and eternity.

With blessings,

The God of Hope Eternal

PSALM 147:11 TLB

His joy is in those who reverence him, those who expect him to be loving and kind.

> ❝ **Be of good courage, and He shall strengthen your heart, all you who hope in the LORD.** ❞
>
> PSALM 31:24 NKJV

Through him you believe in God, who raised him from the dead and glorified him, and so your faith and hope are in God.
1 PETER 1:21 NIV

The LORD is good to those whose hope is in him, to the one who seeks him; it is good to wait quietly for the salvation of the LORD.
LAMENTATIONS 3:25-26 NIV

HEBREWS 10:23
NRSV

Let us hold fast to the confession of our hope without wavering, for he who has promised is faithful.

It is a trustworthy statement deserving full acceptance. For it is for this we labor and strive, because we have fixed our hope on the living God, who is the Savior of all men, especially of believers.
1 TIMOTHY 4:9-10 NAS

I am sure that neither death, nor life, nor angels, nor ruling spirits, nothing now, nothing in the future, no powers, nothing above us, nothing below us, nor anything else in the whole world will ever be able to separate us from the love of God that is in Christ Jesus our Lord.
ROMANS 8:38-39 NCV

Endurance

"We work hard and suffer much in order that people will believe the truth, for our hope is in the living God, who is the Savior of all people, and particularly of those who believe. "

I TIMOTHY 4:10 NLT

Hope does not disappoint, because the love of God has been poured out within our hearts through the Holy Spirit who was given to us.
ROMANS 5:5 NAS

I will sing of your strength, in the morning I will sing of your love; for you are my fortress, my refuge in times of trouble.
PSALM 59:16 NIV

Now may our Lord Jesus Christ himself and God our Father, who loved us and through grace gave us eternal comfort and good hope, comfort your hearts and strengthen them in every good work and word.
2 THESSALONIANS 2:16-17 NRSV

No one shall be able to stand against you all the days of your life. As I was with Moses, so I will be with you; I will not fail you or forsake you.
JOSHUA 1:5 NRSV

66 **You have this faith and love because of your hope, and what you hope for is kept safe for you in heaven. You learned about this hope when you heard the message about the truth, the Good News.** 99

COLOSSIANS 1:5 NCV

No one whose hope is in you will ever be put to shame, but they will be put to shame who are treacherous without excuse.
PSALM 25:3 NIV

The Spirit of the Sovereign LORD is on me, because the LORD has anointed me to preach good news to the poor. He has sent me to bind up the brokenhearted, to proclaim freedom for the captives and release from darkness for the prisoners,
ISAIAH 61:1 NIV

DEUTERONOMY
31:6 MLB

Be strong and courageous; have no fear, nor be at all in dread on their account; for it is the LORD your God who is going with you; He will neither fail you nor forsake you.

O Lord, you are so good and kind, so ready to forgive; so full of mercy for all who ask your aid.
PSALM 86:5 TLB

The LORD has become my stronghold, and my God the rock of my refuge.
PSALM 94:22 NRSV

Endurance

Life's Disappointments

One Whom I Love,

I know that you have struggled at times with disappointment, and you have wondered why I allowed you to endure such painful experiences. I cannot answer your questions now. But I do promise to walk with you through every trial, and I can assure you that those painful circumstances in your life will make you stronger day by day.

Consider an athlete in vigorous training. He pushes his body to the limits almost as if punishing himself. The workouts are hard, exhausting, even painful. The disappointments are many. As he grows stronger, however, he experiences success. Before long, the earlier disappointments fade away. Suddenly all the training seems worthwhile. The athlete has learned endurance. And you, too, My friend, will grow strong as you endure disappointment. One day you will stand victorious, having fulfilled My perfect plan for your life. Then you, too, will see the big picture. Trust Me.

Cheering for you,

Your Biggest Fan

PHILIPPIANS 4:13 NIV

I can do everything through him who gives me strength.

"He gives strength to the weary, and to him who lacks might He increases power. Though youths grow weary and tired, and vigorous young men stumble badly, yet those who wait for the Lᴏʀᴅ will gain new strength; they will mount up with wings like eagles, they will run and not get tired, they will walk and not become weary."

ISAIAH 40:29-31 NAS

You have let me sink down deep in desperate problems. But you will bring me back to life again, up from the depths of the earth. You will give me greater honor than before, and turn again and comfort me.
PSALM 71:20-21 TLB

HEBREWS 10:35 NIV

Do not throw away your confidence; it will be richly rewarded.

Blessed is the man who endures temptation; for when he has been approved, he will receive the crown of life which the Lord has promised to those who love Him.
JAMES 1:12 NKJV

I cry to you, O Lᴏʀᴅ; I say, "You are my refuge, my portion in the land of the living."
PSALM 142:5 NRSV

Endurance

shine on

Dear Bright and Shining One,

Yes, you are like a lamp. And when I see you glowing, it makes Me smile. But like a lamp, you need a fuel source to keep your light shining bright. I am your source.

That's right, My friend, your power must come from Me. Like an electric lamp that needs a source of energy, you must be plugged into Me. For without Me you may be a nice-looking lamp, but no light will flow through you. And when the night is dark, what use is the loveliest lamp if it gives no light?

Remain connected to Me, your energy source, and I will shine right through you. Amazing things will happen! The darkness in your life will disappear, and your light will brighten the path for others as well. So shine on!

Your power source,

The Light of the World

2 SAMUEL 22:29 TLB

O Lord, you are my light! You make my darkness bright.

"You are the light of the world. A city on a hill cannot be hidden. Neither do people light a lamp and put it under a bowl. Instead they put it on its stand, and it gives light to everyone in the house. In the same way, let your light shine before men, that they may see your good deeds and praise your Father in heaven."

MATTHEW 5:14-16 NIV

You are a chosen people, a royal priesthood, a holy nation, a people belonging to God, that you may declare the praises of him who called you out of darkness into his wonderful light.

1 PETER 2:9 NIV

PSALM 27:1 TLB

The Lord is my light and my salvation... whom shall I fear?

Jesus came and told his disciples,"I have been given complete authority in heaven and on earth. Therefore, go and make disciples of all the nations, baptizing them in the name of the Father and the Son and the Holy Spirit. Teach these new disciples to obey all the commands I have given you. And be sure of this: I am with you always, even to the end of the age."

MATTHEW 28:18-20 NLT

Spreading Light

Obedient Hearts

Dear Friend,

The word obedience is not very popular these days. But if you are wise, you will choose to obey Me by honoring My commandments and listening to My voice deep inside your heart. At times I will ask you to step out in faith and do what I tell you without explanation.

Remember, I would never ask you to do anything that would cause harm to you or to others. That is not My way of doing things. My intention is to keep you safe and headed toward a successful, fulfilled life. I see so much more than you are able to see. That's why you must trust My judgment calls and strive to live in obedience to My laws. I assure you, I only have your best interest in mind.

One of the most meaningful forms of obedience begins in your heart and is motivated by your love for Me. My happiest moments are when you look to Me and eagerly say, "Yes, God!" Oh, how it makes Me proud! I know that you are learning to really trust Me. So please, try to understand that obedience is for your own good and that it is the very best when wrapped in love!

Lovingly,

Your Heavenly Father

PSALM 106:3 NIV

Blessed are they who maintain justice, who constantly do what is right.

❝The one who obeys me is the one who loves me; and because he loves me, my Father will love him; and I will too, and I will reveal myself to him.❞

JOHN 14:21 TLB

The world is passing away, and the lust of it; but he who does the will of God abides forever.
1 JOHN 2:17 NKJV

Because he has loved Me, therefore I will deliver him; I will set him securely on high, because he has known My name.
PSALM 91:14 NAS

JOB 36:11 NLT

If they listen and obey God, then they will be blessed with prosperity throughout their lives. All their years will be pleasant.

You shall walk in all the ways which the LORD your God has commanded you, that you may live and that it may be well with you, and that you may prolong your days in the land which you shall possess.
DEUTERONOMY 5:33 NKJV

Trust the Lord and sincerely worship him; think of all the tremendous things he has done for you.
1 SAMUEL 12:24 TLB

Obedience

Improve Your Serve

Dear Friend,

Few people aspire to become servants these days. In the world's eyes, a servant is about the lowest position a person can have. But not in My opinion. For when My Son came to earth, He came to serve and lay down His life for others. By doing so, He set a marvelous example.

I encourage you to learn to serve others with a cheerful heart. Practice serving those around you; be the one who encourages others; quietly help someone else succeed. Get in the habit of stepping aside and letting someone else go first. Don't try to be the center of attention.

When you do these things, know that I am watching and smiling down upon you and getting ready to lift you up!

With love,

The King of Kings

2 CORINTHIANS 9:7 NAS

Each one must do just as he has purposed in his heart, not grudgingly or under compulsion, for God loves a cheerful giver.

> **"Whoever wants to become great among you must be your servant, and whoever wants to be first must be your slave—just as the Son of Man did not come to be served, but to serve, and to give his life as a ransom for many."**
>
> MATTHEW 20:26-28 NIV

God blesses those who are kind to the poor. He helps them out of their troubles. He protects them and keeps them alive; he publicly honors them and destroys the power of their enemies.
PSALM 41:1-2 TLB

HEBREWS 13:2 NLT

Don't forget to show hospitality to strangers, for some who have done this have entertained angels without realizing it!

If anyone gives even a cup of cold water to one of these little ones because he is my disciple, I tell you the truth, he will certainly not lose his reward.
MATTHEW 10:42 NIV

Do not withhold good from those who deserve it, when it is in your power to act.
PROVERBS 3:27 NIV

Contribute to the needs of the saints; extend hospitality to strangers.
ROMANS 12:13 NRSV

Service

> **If anyone serves Me, let him follow Me; and where I am, there My servant will be also. If anyone serves Me, him My Father will honor.**
>
> JOHN 12:26 NKJV

If I then, your Lord and Teacher, have washed your feet, you also ought to wash one another's feet. For I have given you an example, that you should do as I have done to you. Most assuredly, I say to you, a servant is not greater than his master; nor is he who is sent greater than he who sent him.
JOHN 13:14-16 NKJV

I tell you the truth, a servant is not greater than his master. A messenger is not greater than the one who sent him.
JOHN 13:16 NCV

Pure and lasting religion in the sight of God our Father means that we must care for orphans and widows in their troubles, and refuse to let the world corrupt us.
JAMES 1:27 NLT

Don't forget about those in jail. Suffer with them as though you were there yourself. Share the sorrow of those being mistreated, for you know what they are going through.
HEBREWS 13:3 TLB

Improve Your Serve

> **"Of this gospel I have become a servant according to the gift of God's grace that was given me by the working of his power."**
>
> EPHESIANS 3:7 NRSV

Whoever wants to become great among you must be your servant, and whoever wants to be first must be slave of all.
MARK 10:43-44 NIV

Look down and have mercy on me. Give strength to your servant; yes, save me, for I am your servant.
PSALM 86:16 NLT

GALATIANS 1:10 TLB

You can see that I am not trying to please you by sweet talk and flattery; no, I am trying to please God. If I were still trying to please men I could not be Christ's servant.

Let him who is the greatest among you become as the youngest, and the leader as the servant.
LUKE 22:26 NAS

If the poor are hated even by their kin, how much more are they shunned by their friends!
PROVERBS 19:7 NRSV

Do not neglect to do good and to share what you have, for such sacrifices are pleasing to God.
HEBREWS 13:16 NRSV

Service

Fighting Fear

Dear Friend,

I know you struggle with fear from time to time. Everyone does. Fear is a part of living on this planet. But fear, left to itself, can have a devastating effect. It can grow like a cancer, strip the fun from your life, and paralyze you with its power. That kind of fear never comes from Me.

How can you escape fear's evil clutches? How can you turn your back on it and be free from its thorny grasp? Once again, the answer is found in your relationship with Me. When you begin to accept My love for you, your fears will start to fade away. When you realize how deeply I care for you, how I long to protect you, how vast is My love for you, those old fears will simply flee.

Fear cannot exist in the presence of My perfect love. My love is like a bright beacon of light that immediately dispels the darkness of fear. Draw near, My friend; bask in the light of My love, and just watch as fear melts away.

In power and love,

The Almighty

2 TIMOTHY 1:7 NKJV

For God has not given us a spirit of fear, but of power and of love and of a sound mind.

> " I, the LORD your God, will hold your right hand, saying to you, 'Fear not, I will help you.' "
>
> ISAIAH 41:13 NKJV

We need have no fear of someone who loves us perfectly; his perfect love for us eliminates all dread of what he might do to us. If we are afraid, it is for fear of what he might do to us, and shows that we are not fully convinced that he really loves us.

1 JOHN 4:18 TLB

JOHN 14:27 NIV

Peace I leave with you; my peace I give you. I do not give to you as the world gives. Do not let your hearts be troubled and do not be afraid.

The LORD is my light and my salvation; whom shall I fear? The LORD is the defense of my life; whom shall I dread? When evildoers came upon me to devour my flesh, my adversaries and my enemies, they stumbled and fell. Though a host encamp against me, my heart will not fear; though war arise against me, in spite of this I shall be confident.

PSALM 27:1-3 NAS

Be joyful because you have hope. Be patient when trouble comes, and pray at all times.

ROMANS 12:12 NCV

Courage

> **You can sleep without fear; you need not be afraid of disaster or the plots of wicked men, for the Lord is with you; he protects you.**
>
> PROVERBS 3:24-26 TLB

In all these things we are more than conquerors through him who loved us. For I am convinced that neither death nor life, neither angels nor demons, neither the present nor the future, nor any powers, neither height nor depth, nor anything else in all creation, will be able to separate us from the love of God that is in Christ Jesus our Lord.
ROMANS 8:37-39 NIV

Whenever you face trials of any kind, consider it nothing but joy, because you know that the testing of your faith produces endurance; and let endurance have its full effect, so that you may be mature and complete, lacking in nothing.
JAMES 1:2-4 NRSV

Be alert; stand firm in the faith; play the man; be strong.
1 CORINTHIANS 16:13 MLB

Do not be afraid of them. Remember the Lord, great and awesome, and fight for your brethren, your sons, your daughters, your wives, and your houses.
NEHEMIAH 4:14 NKJV

> **" Even if you should suffer for what is right, you are blessed. 'Do not fear what they fear; do not be frightened.' "**

I PETER 3:14 NIV

Their ships are tossed to the heavens and sink again to the depths; the sailors cringe in terror. They reel and stagger like drunkards and are at their wit's end. Then they cry to the Lord in their trouble, and he saves them. He calms the storm and stills the waves. What a blessing is that stillness, as he brings them safely into harbor!

PSALM 107:26-30 TLB

PSALM 31:15 NLT

My future is in your hands. Rescue me from those who hunt me down relentlessly.

You have not received a spirit of slavery leading to fear again, but you have received a spirit of adoption as sons by which we cry out, "Abba! Father!"

ROMANS 8:15 NAS

Be strong and courageous; do not be frightened or dismayed, for the LORD your God is with you wherever you go.

JOSHUA 1:9 NRSV

Courage

Dear Friend,

I haven't said much about My adversary, but I will now so that you will be able to defend yourself against him. Even though My Son defeated him when He rose from the dead, our delusional enemy hasn't yet given up the fight. He roams the earth, making trouble for those who belong to Me. So be wise and prepared to deal with him.

I encourage you to protect yourself with the following spiritual weapons: My truth can fend off the enemy's lies. And faith in Me is like a shield, which can protect your heart from his assaults. My peace can guide your feet through any battlefield. Allow Me to equip you for the challenges that lie ahead, and together we can enjoy great victories.

With all authority,

Your Victorious Leader

Be Brave

EPHESIANS 6:11 NKJV

Put on the whole armor of God, that you may be able to stand against the wiles of the devil.

"The night is nearly over; the day is almost here. So let us put aside the deeds of darkness and put on the armor of light."

ROMANS 13:12 NIV

Since we are of the day, let us be sober, having put on the breastplate of faith and love, and as a helmet, the hope of salvation.
1 THESSALONIANS 5:8 NAS

He is my strength, my shield from every danger. I trusted in him, and he helped me. Joy rises in my heart until I burst out in songs of praise to him.
PSALM 28:7 TLB

PSALM 112:7 NAS

He will not fear evil tidings; his heart is steadfast, trusting in the LORD.

In your strength I can scale any wall, attack any troop.
PSALM 18:29 TLB

The Lord GOD will help Me; therefore I will not be disgraced; therefore I have set My face like a flint, and I know that I will not be ashamed.
ISAIAH 50:7 NKJV

Do not be terrified by them, for the LORD your God, who is among you, is a great and awesome God.
DEUTERONOMY 7:21 NIV

Armor

The Helper

Dear Friend,

You are not strong enough to withstand all of life's trials on your own, and for that reason I have sent My Holy Spirit. Some call Him the Helper.

But just so you'll understand, My Holy Spirit and My Son Jesus are both part of Me. All three of us (the Father, the Son, and the Holy Spirit) are actually One. I know that's confusing, so let Me give an illustration to help you better understand. Consider one man who is someone's father; but he is also someone's son; and he's also someone's brother. Father, son, brother—three different roles interacting in three different ways. Yet there is only one man. That's similar to Me.

The role of My Holy Spirit is to live inside you. Sometimes you hear His quiet voice whispering truth deep within your heart. He is the One who can comfort and encourage you. And He can lead and guide you toward what is good and right. Listen to Him.

In power and might,

The Giver of Every Good and Perfect Gift

EZEKIEL 36:26 TLB

I will give you a new heart—I will give you new and right desires—and put a new spirit within you. I will take out your stony hearts of sin and give you new hearts of love.

> **The Spirit of God has made me, and the breath of the Almighty gives me life.**
>
> JOB 33:4 NKJV

Repent, and each of you be baptized in the name of Jesus Christ for the forgiveness of your sins; and you will receive the gift of the Holy Spirit. For the promise is for you and your children and for all who are far off, as many as the Lord our God will call to Himself.

ACTS 2:38-39 NAS

2 PETER 1:20-21 TLB

No prophecy recorded in Scripture was ever thought up by the prophet himself. It was the Holy Spirit within these godly men who gave them true messages from God.

If you then, though you are evil, know how to give good gifts to your children, how much more will your Father in heaven give the Holy Spirit to those who ask him!

LUKE 11:13 NIV

You will receive power when the Holy Spirit comes on you; and you will be my witnesses in Jerusalem, and in all Judea and Samaria, and to the ends of the earth.

ACTS 1:8 NIV

Holy Spirit

The Helper

"In the last days," God said, "I will pour out my Holy Spirit upon all mankind, and your sons and daughters shall prophesy, and your young men shall see visions, and your old men dream dreams."
ACTS 2:17 TLB

Hope does not disappoint us, because God has poured out his love into our hearts by the Holy Spirit, whom he has given us.
ROMANS 5:5 NIV

I will pray the Father, and He will give you another Helper, that He may abide with you forever—the Spirit of truth, whom the world cannot receive, because it neither sees Him nor knows Him; but you know Him, for He dwells with you and will be in you.
JOHN 14:16-17 NKJV

Do you not know that your body is a temple of the Holy Spirit, who is in you, whom you have received from God? You are not your own.

I CORINTHIANS 6:19 NIV

"As for me, this is my promise to them," says the Lord: "My Holy Spirit shall not leave them, and they shall want the good and hate the wrong—they and their children and their children's children forever."

ISAIAH 59:21 TLB

JOHN 16:7 NAS

I tell you the truth, it is to your advantage that I go away; for if I do not go away, the Helper will not come to you; but if I go, I will send Him to you.

When the Helper comes, whom I shall send to you from the Father, the Spirit of truth who proceeds from the Father, He will testify of Me.

JOHN 15:26 NKJV

Now I will send the Holy Spirit upon you, just as my Father promised. Don't begin telling others yet—stay here in the city until the Holy Spirit comes and fills you with power from heaven.

LUKE 24:49 TLB

Holy Spirit

Real Romance

Dear Loved One,

I know how you long for a soul mate, someone to love you and to be loved by you. These physical and emotional longings are natural. It is how I designed you. Yet too often, I watch people rush into romantic relationships without thinking. Before they realize it, things have become too serious—emotions get tangled, intense pressures rise, and expectations become unrealistic.

That's how people get hurt. Because I love you, I want to spare you that kind of pain. I want to protect you from the heartbreak of "falling in love" and becoming physically involved too soon.

I would encourage you not to be hasty. Don't give your heart away to the first person you feel drawn to. Be careful not to rush into a commitment you are not yet ready to make. Don't be afraid to wait for the right person and the right time. If you are wise, you will find that love and marriage are two of the most beautiful experiences life has to offer and well worth the investment of time it takes to be sure.

Most lovingly,

Your Heavenly Father

MATTHEW 26:41 NKJV

Watch and pray, lest you enter into temptation. The spirit indeed is willing, but the flesh is weak.

"No temptation has seized you except what is common to man. And God is faithful; he will not let you be tempted beyond what you can bear. But when you are tempted, he will also provide a way out so that you can stand up under it."

I CORINTHIANS 10:13 NIV

The grace of God has appeared, bringing salvation to all men, instructing us to deny ungodliness and worldly desires and to live sensibly, righteously and godly in the present age.

TITUS 2:11-12 NAS

2 TIMOTHY 3:10 NAS

You followed my teaching, conduct, purpose, faith, patience, love, perseverance.

Remember, when someone wants to do wrong it is never God who is tempting him, for God never wants to do wrong and never tempts anyone else to do it.

JAMES 1:13 TLB

Patience develops strength of character in us and helps us trust God more each time we use it until finally our hope and faith are strong and steady.

ROMANS 5:4 TLB

We show we are servants of God by our pure lives, our understanding, patience, and kindness, by the Holy Spirit, by true love.

2 CORINTHIANS 6:6 NCV

Romance

Resting Place

My Own,

This old world can make people weary. I can see how some days you feel that you have too much to bear. Don't worry. I understand all about that, and I don't view this as any personal flaw on your part—not at all! I view this as an opportunity.

When the world wears you down and you feel tired, consider it a signal, a reminder that you need to come to Me, for I am the One who can give you rest—real rest. Only I know the deepest needs of your trail-worn soul, and only I can meet those needs.

But even more than merely giving you rest, I can walk alongside you and show you ways that will lighten your load. I can teach you how to pace yourself, how to discern what is and what isn't a good use of your time and energy.

I invite you; come to Me. Enjoy the rest I have for you.

Assuredly yours,

The One Who Made You

JEREMIAH 31:25 NAS

For I satisfy the weary ones and refresh everyone who languishes.

> **❝I will both lie down in peace, and sleep; For You alone, O LORD, make me dwell in safety.❞**
>
> PSALM 4:8 NKJV

Yet the Lord pleads with you still: Ask where the good road is, the godly paths you used to walk in, in the days of long ago. Travel there, and you will find rest for your souls.
JEREMIAH 6:16 TLB

For I am like a tree whose roots reach the water, whose branches are refreshed with the dew.
JOB 29:19 NLT

PSALM 126:4 TLB

May we be refreshed as by streams in the desert.

Your love has given me great joy and encouragement, because you, brother, have refreshed the hearts of the saints.
PHILEMON 7 NIV

It is a sign between Me and the sons of Israel forever; for in six days the LORD made heaven and earth, but on the seventh day He ceased from labor, and was refreshed.
EXODUS 31:17 NAS

Rest

Resting Place

God, you sent much rain;
you refreshed your tired land.
PSALM 68:9 NCV

My people will live in a peaceful
habitation, and in secure dwellings
and in undisturbed resting places.
ISAIAH 32:18 NAS

My presence will go with you, and I
will give you rest.
EXODUS 33:14 NRSV

Thou art my hiding place; Thou wilt
preserve me from trouble, Thou wilt
surround me with songs of
deliverance.
PSALM 32:7 MLB

God is our refuge and strength, a
tested help in times of trouble. And
so we need not fear even if the world
blows up, and the mountains
crumble into the sea.
PSALM 46:1-2 TLB

> **" So I said, 'Oh, that I had wings like a dove! I would fly away and be at rest.' "**
>
> PSALM 55:6 NKJV

For this reason we have been comforted. And besides our comfort, we rejoiced even much more for the joy of Titus, because his spirit has been refreshed by you all.
2 CORINTHIANS 7:13 NAS

Let us do our best to go into that place of rest, too, being careful not to disobey God as the children of Israel did, thus failing to get in.
HEBREWS 4:11 TLB

PROVERBS 3:24
NRSV

If you sit down, you will not be afraid; when you lie down, your sleep will be sweet.

I am leaving you with a gift—peace of mind and heart. And the peace I give isn't like the peace the world gives. So don't be troubled or afraid.
JOHN 14:27 NLT

God who cheers those who are discouraged refreshed us by the arrival of Titus.
2 CORINTHIANS 7:6 TLB

Let the peace of Christ rule in your hearts, to which indeed you were called in the one body.
COLOSSIANS 3:15 NRSV

Rest

Remember, all the things of this world will one day pass away.

Love of Money

Dear Friend,

I want to talk to you about an important matter—money. It's important because it can pose a real danger to your life and well-being. Money is not bad in and of itself. But it does have the potential to pull your attention away from the right path and lead down a road headed for loneliness and destruction. Unless you are careful, money can become the most important thing in your life, destroying important relationships, causing you to abandon your values, and pulling you far away from Me.

I'd like to spare you that. So here are a few things to keep in mind: I am the One who provides for you; all that you have comes from Me. If you remember these things, you will be less likely to fret and worry unnecessarily, or even to hoard money because of unfounded fears. Of course, I do want you to be responsible and a good steward of what I give you, but don't hold on too tightly. Remember that generosity and giving are great ways to prevent greed. And don't forget that all earthly things will one day pass away. So focus your heart on what really matters—the things of the Spirit.

Meeting all your needs,

The Great Provider

HEBREWS 13:5 NIV

Keep your lives free from the love of money and be content with what you have, because God has said, "Never will I leave you; never will I forsake you."

150

> **"Give, and it will be given to you: good measure, pressed down, shaken together, and running over will be put into your bosom. For with the same measure that you use, it will be measured back to you."**
>
> LUKE 6:38 NKJV

If someone who is supposed to be a Christian has money enough to live well, and sees a brother in need, and won't help him—how can God's love be within him?
1 JOHN 3:17 TLB

PROVERBS 28:27
TLB

If you give to the poor, your needs will be supplied! But a curse upon those who close their eyes to poverty.

He said to them, "Beware, and be on your guard against every form of greed; for not even when one has an abundance does his life consist of his possessions."
LUKE 12:15 NAS

He called His disciples to Himself and said to them, "Assuredly, I say to you that this poor widow has put in more than all those who have given to the treasury; for they all put in out of their abundance, but she out of her poverty put in all that she had, her whole livelihood."
MARK 12:43-44 NKJV

Priorities

Way to Worship

Dear Friend,

Some people think I'm egotistical because I encourage your praises and exaltations. And that makes Me smile. For, although I dearly love to hear My children worship Me, there is a much bigger reason I delight in your praises. Would you like to know why worship is so important?

You see, I designed the human spirit with a deep inner longing to praise. Unfortunately this can lead some people (those who don't yet realize that I alone am God) to worship the wrong things. But mostly, this need to worship eventually draws people to Me. And when they praise Me, they experience My glory and majesty. That makes their hearts joyous and light.

Ultimately, praise will cause you to turn your eyes away from your own problems and focus on Me, the source of all your answers. It will remind you that all the resources of Almighty God are available to you. And it will assure you that I am always with you! I watch as your face fills with joy. I sense your spirit growing lighter and your sadness slipping away like a cloak from your shoulders.

So you see, worship is a wonderful thing—not just for Me, but also for you!

Most joyously,

The Exalted One

JOHN 4:24 NIV

God is spirit, and his worshipers must worship in spirit and in truth.

"Oh come, let us worship and bow down; let us kneel before the LORD our Maker. For He is our God, and we are the people of His pasture, and the sheep of His hand."

PSALM 95:6-7 NKJV

The Lord is my strength, my song, and my salvation. He is my God, and I will praise him. He is my father's God—I will exalt him.
EXODUS 15:2 TLB

I will give You thanks forever, because You have done it, and I will wait on Your name, for it is good, in the presence of Your godly ones.
PSALM 52:9 NAS

PSALM 47:1-2 NKJV

Oh, clap your hands, all you peoples! Shout to God with the voice of triumph! For the LORD Most High is awesome; He is a great King over all the earth.

Praise his name with dancing, accompanied by drums and lyre.
PSALM 149:3 TLB

Because your steadfast love is better than life, my lips will praise you. So I will bless you as long as I live; I will lift up my hands and call on your name.
PSALM 63:3-4 NRSV

Worship

> **"Since we are receiving a kingdom that cannot be shaken, let us be thankful, and so worship God acceptably with reverence and awe."**
>
> HEBREWS 12:28 NIV

Way to Worship

The twenty-four elders fall down before him who sits on the throne, and worship him who lives for ever and ever. They lay their crowns before the throne and say: "You are worthy, our Lord and God, to receive glory and honor and power, for you created all things, and by your will they were created and have their being."
REVELATION 4:10-11 NIV

I will thank you, LORD, with all my heart; I will tell of all the marvelous things you have done. I will be filled with joy because of you. I will sing praises to your name, O Most High.
PSALM 9:1-2 NLT

Fear God and give him glory, for the hour of his judgment has come; and worship him who made heaven and earth, the sea and the springs of water.
REVELATION 14:7 NRSV

I will praise the name of God with a song; I will magnify him with thanksgiving.
PSALM 69:30 NRSV

> **"Jesus replied, 'We must worship God, and him alone. So it is written in the Scriptures.'"**
>
> LUKE 4.0 TLB

We who worship God in the Spirit are the only ones who are truly circumcised. We put no confidence in human effort. Instead, we boast about what Christ Jesus has done for us.
PHILIPPIANS 3:3 NLT

The secret things in their hearts will be made known. So they will bow down and worship God saying, "Truly, God is with you."
1 CORINTHIANS 14:25 NCV

PSALM 146:2 NIV

I will praise the LORD all my life; I will sing praise to my God as long as I live.

I will rejoice in the LORD,
I will joy in the God of my salvation.
The LORD God is my strength;
He will make my feet like deer's feet,
and He will make me walk on my high hills.
HABAKKUK 3:18-19 NKJV

The LORD lives; blessed be my rock, and exalted be the God of my salvation.
PSALM 18:46 MLB

Worship

Resisting Wrong

Dear Loved One,

This world is full of temptation, but don't despair. Temptation can serve a purpose. As you learn to resist temptation, you become strong enough to stand against even bigger trials that will come in the future. It's like resistance training—the more you work out, the stronger you become.

One key to resisting temptation is to recognize it quickly. Temptation is tricky. It may seem good rather than harmful. But I am always here to help. Ask Me. For I can teach you how to recognize temptation and show you ways to resist it.

Keep your heart tuned to Me, and practice hearing My quiet voice deep within. I will always warn you when temptation is ready to strike. So keep your ears and eyes open, and set your heart to obey.

Always here for you,

The Great I Am

MATTHEW 6:13 NIV

Lead us not into temptation, but deliver us from the evil one.

"We do not have a high priest who cannot sympathize with our weaknesses, but One who has been tempted in all things as we are, yet without sin."

HEBREWS 4:15 NAS

Keep alert and pray. Otherwise temptation will overpower you. For the spirit indeed is willing, but how weak the body is!
MATTHEW 26:41 TLB

Let him who thinks he stands take heed lest he fall. No temptation has overtaken you except such as is common to man; but God is faithful, who will not allow you to be tempted beyond what you are able, but with the temptation will also make the way of escape, that you may be able to bear it.
1 CORINTHIANS 10:12-13 NKJV

LUKE 22:40 TLB

He told them, "Pray God that you will not be overcome by temptation."

Since he himself has gone through suffering and temptation, he is able to help us when we are being tempted.
HEBREWS 2:18 NLT

The Lord knows how to rescue the godly from temptation, and to keep the unrighteous under punishment for the day of judgment.
2 PETER 2:9 NAS

Temptation

Don't Worry

My Special One,

It is the way of this world to worry and fret over many things. More and more it seems that some people enjoy preying upon the anxieties of others. I have seen how small concerns can be blown out of proportion, causing fear and distress to prevail in the hearts and minds of those who listen and watch.

This is not how I want you to live. Heightened anxiety and stress can drain your spirit and weaken you, stripping away happiness and joy. Instead of worrying, I encourage you to pray. Yes, come to Me about everything that concerns you!

Remember, I am your Heavenly Father. What is too great or too difficult for Me? Nothing can overcome you when you rest safely in My hands. Do not forget that I, the Lord God, take excellent care of you, and don't forget that I can see you through anything. Don't worry or be anxious. Trust Me and pray!

Always here for you,

The Lord God Almighty

PSALM 9:9 NAS

The LORD also will be a stronghold for the oppressed, a stronghold in times of trouble.

159

> **You are my hiding place; You shall preserve me from trouble; You shall surround me with songs of deliverance.**

PSALM 32:7 NKJV

We know that in all things God works for the good of those who love him, who have been called according to his purpose.
ROMANS 8:28 NIV

When he calls on me I will answer; I will be with him in trouble, and rescue him and honor him.
PSALM 91:15 TLB

JOHN 14:1 TLB

Let not your heart be troubled. You are trusting God, now trust in me.

My God will meet all your needs according to his glorious riches in Christ Jesus.
PHILIPPIANS 4:19 NIV

Be anxious for nothing, but in everything by prayer and supplication, with thanksgiving, let your requests be made known to God; and the peace of God, which surpasses all understanding, will guard your hearts and minds through Christ Jesus.
PHILIPPIANS 4:6-7 NKJV

Trust

Don't Worry

Patience develops strength of character in us and helps us trust God more each time we use it until finally our hope and faith are strong and steady.
ROMANS 5:4 TLB

Some trust in chariots, others in horses, but we trust the LORD our God.
PSALM 20:7 NCV

Cast your burden on the LORD, and He shall sustain you; He shall never permit the righteous to be moved.
PSALM 55:22 NKJV

When I am afraid, I will trust in you. In God, whose word I praise, in God I trust; I will not be afraid. What can mortal man do to me?
PSALM 56:3-4 NIV

Let not your heart be troubled. You are trusting God, now trust in me.
JOHN 14:1 TLB

"Don't be troubled. You trust God, now trust in me."

JOHN 14.1 NLT

So they would all trust God and would not forget what he had done but would obey his commands.
PSALM 78:7 NCV

Only we who believe God can enter into his place of rest. He has said, "I have sworn in my anger that those who don't believe me will never get in," even though he has been ready and waiting for them since the world began.
HEBREWS 4:3 TLB

ACTS 27:25 NLT

So take courage! For I believe God. It will be just as he said.

I praise God for his word. I trust God, so I am not afraid. What can human beings do to me?
PSALM 56:4 NCV

The LORD has become my stronghold, and my God the rock of my refuge.
PSALM 94:22 NRSV

Those of steadfast mind you keep in peace—in peace because they trust in you.
ISAIAH 26:3 NRSV

Trust

Lukewarm Living

One Whom I Love,

A lot of apathy is floating around these days, especially among the young people whom I love so dearly. This concerns Me. For apathy and indifference are just another way of saying "I don't care," and not caring is a very dangerous thing.

I would prefer that a person be cold and hard and dead-set against Me than to merely not care. For I can readily warm a cold heart, but the person who doesn't care has surrendered his or her power to respond. Please don't let your heart become this way. My desire is for you to be filled with heat and passion and love toward Me. Great things can be accomplished through a person with a passion to do right and follow in My ways.

So, My friend, I invite you to live fully and draw near to Me. Allow Me to fan the flame in your heart. Come to Me, and your commitment toward Me will burn steadfastly and with great intensity!

Passionately,

The Lover of
Your Soul

REVELATION 3:16 NAS

Because you are lukewarm, and neither hot nor cold, I will spit you out of My mouth.

> ❝The eyes of the LORD range throughout the earth to strengthen those whose hearts are fully committed to him.❞
>
> 2 CHRONICLES 16:9 NIV

[When I return] the world will be [as indifferent to the things of God] as the people were in Noah's day.
LUKE 17:26 TLB

If a man makes a vow to the LORD, or swears an oath to bind himself by some agreement, he shall not break his word; he shall do according to all that proceeds out of his mouth.
NUMBERS 30:2 NKJV

2 CORINTHIANS 8:7 NKJV

As you abound in everything—in faith, in speech, in knowledge, in all diligence, and in your love for us—see that you abound in this grace also.

Commit yourself to the LORD; let Him deliver him; let Him rescue him, because He delights in him.
PSALM 22:8 NAS

Today the LORD your God has commanded you to obey all these laws and regulations. You must commit yourself to them without reservation.
DEUTERONOMY 26:16 NLT

You became our followers and the Lord's; for you received our message with joy from the Holy Spirit in spite of the trials and sorrows it brought you.
1 THESSALONIANS 1:6 TLB

Passion

True Riches

My Treasured One,

You are My treasure! You are worth more to Me than a mountain of pure gold topped with flawless diamonds. For you see, I understand what is truly precious and valuable. I know what sort of riches are imperishable and lasting, and I long for you to begin to see the difference as well.

One way to quickly realize the value of something is to ask, "What will this be worth to me a hundred years from now?" If it's a material possession it will most likely be worth nothing to you by then, for you will probably be gone from this earth! But spiritual matters or meaningful personal relationships have lasting value—these are true riches.

Learn to distinguish what is of real value and what is not. Then learn to treasure those portions of life that are truly priceless and irreplaceable. They are the riches on which you should set your heart.

With wisdom and love,

The Lord of All

MATTHEW 6:24 TLB

You cannot serve two masters: God and money. For you will hate one and love the other, or else the other way around.

❝Wisdom and knowledge will be the stability of your times, and the strength of salvation; the fear of the LORD is His treasure.❞

ISAIAH 33:6 NKJV

Do not store up for yourselves treasures on earth, where moth and rust destroy, and where thieves break in and steal. But store up for yourselves treasures in heaven, where moth and rust do not destroy, and where thieves do not break in and steal. For where your treasure is, there your heart will be also.
MATTHEW 6:19-21 NIV

I CORINTHIANS 1:3 NLT

May God our Father and the Lord Jesus Christ give you his grace and peace.

That their hearts may be encouraged, having been knit together in love, and attaining to all the wealth that comes from the full assurance of understanding, resulting in a true knowledge of God's mystery, that is, Christ Himself, in whom are hidden all the treasures of wisdom and knowledge.
COLOSSIANS 2:2-3 NAS

In Him, who is the head of all rule and authority, you are enjoying fullness of life.
COLOSSIANS 2:10 MLB

Treasure

True Riches

When Jesus heard this, he said to him, "You still lack one thing. Sell everything you have and give to the poor, and you will have treasure in heaven. Then come, follow me."
LUKE 18:22 NIV

By doing that, they will be saving a treasure for themselves as a strong foundation for the future. Then they will be able to have the life that is true life.
1 TIMOTHY 6:19 NCV

Jesus said to him, "If you wish to be complete, go and sell your possessions and give to the poor, and you will have treasure in heaven; and come, follow Me."
MATTHEW 19:21 NAS

It is from God alone that you have your life through Christ Jesus. He showed us God's plan of salvation; he was the one who made us acceptable to God; he made us pure and holy and gave himself to purchase our salvation.
1 CORINTHIANS 1:30 TLB

"Guard the good treasure entrusted to you, with the help of the Holy Spirit living in us."

2 TIMOTHY 1:14 NRSV

The Kingdom of Heaven is like a treasure that a man discovered hidden in a field. In his excitement, he hid it again and sold everything he owned to get enough money to buy the field—and to get the treasure, too!
MATTHEW 13:44 NLT

We have this treasure in earthen vessels, that the excellence of the power may be of God and not of us.
2 CORINTHIANS 4:7 NKJV

LUKE 12:33 NIV

Sell your possessions and give to the poor. Provide purses for yourselves that will not wear out, a treasure in heaven that will not be exhausted, where no thief comes near and no moth destroys.

Yes, if you want better insight and discernment, and are searching for them as you would for lost money or hidden treasure, then wisdom will be given you, and knowledge of God himself; you will soon learn the importance of reverence for the Lord and of trusting him.
PROVERBS 2:3-5 TLB

How lovely is your dwelling place, O LORD of hosts! My soul longs, indeed it faints for the courts of the LORD; my heart and my flesh sing for joy to the living God.
PSALM 84:1-2 NRSV

Treasure

Knowing and Doing

Dear Friend,

I hope you are growing in wisdom and strength. Like a proud Father, I look forward to your progress. Each day I want you to draw closer to Me. For I long to direct you and reveal My will for specific areas of your life. I am delighted when you listen to My voice. I want you to know what it is I'm calling you to do.

But knowing My will and doing it are two different things. Sometimes you do know what I expect, but it's difficult for you to actually follow through. You suddenly want to rebel against My voice and seek your own way. But don't be too disheartened, for it's all part of the human condition. I am understanding and forgiving. When you realize you have blown it, just turn around and come back to Me.

In time you will learn not only to know My will, but also to do it. For that is how you will become all that I have called you to be and accomplish every detail of My perfect plan for your life.

Because I love you,

Your Heavenly Father

I JOHN 2:17 NIV

The world and its desires pass away, but the man who does the will of God lives forever.

"With all the earnestness I have I tell you this—no one who obeys me shall ever die!"

JOHN 8:51 TLB

The things you have learned and received and heard and seen in me, practice these things, and the God of peace will be with you.
PHILIPPIANS 4:9 NAS

If they obey and serve Him, they shall spend their days in prosperity, and their years in pleasures.
JOB 36:11 NKJV

JOHN 15:10 NIV

If you obey my commands, you will remain in my love, just as I have obeyed my Father's commands and remain in his love.

You shall keep my statutes and my ordinances; by doing so one shall live: I am the LORD.
LEVITICUS 18:5 NRSV

Blessed are the undefiled in the way, who walk in the law of the LORD! Blessed are those who keep His testimonies, who seek Him with the whole heart!
PSALM 119:1-2 NKJV

My Will

> **"It is God's will that your good lives should silence those who make foolish accusations against you."**
>
> 1 PETER 2:15 NLT

For this reason, since the day we heard it, we have not ceased praying for you and asking that you may be filled with the knowledge of God's will in all spiritual wisdom and understanding.
COLOSSIANS 1:9 NRSV

Help me to do your will,
for you are my God.
Lead me in good paths,
for your Spirit is good.
PSALM 143:10 TLB

Remember, it is a message to obey, not just to listen to. If you don't obey, you are only fooling yourself. For if you just listen and don't obey, it is like looking at your face in a mirror but doing nothing to improve your appearance. You see yourself, walk away, and forget what you look like. But if you keep looking steadily into God's perfect law—the law that sets you free—and if you do what it says and don't forget what you heard, then God will bless you for doing it.
JAMES 1:22-25 NLT

> **"Lead me in the path of your commands, because that makes me happy."**
>
> PSALM 119:35 NCV

Patient endurance is what you need now, so you will continue to do God's will. Then you will receive all that he has promised.
HEBREWS 10:36 NLT

You are free from the law, but that doesn't mean you are free to do wrong. Live as those who are free to do only God's will at all times.
1 PETER 2:16 TLB

JOHN 7:17 NIV

If anyone chooses to do God's will, he will find out whether my teaching comes from God or whether I speak on my own.

Anyone who does God's will is my brother, and my sister, and my mother.
MARK 3:35 TLB

When the Spirit of truth comes, he will lead you into all truth. He will not speak his own words, but he will speak only what he hears, and he will tell you what is to come.
JOHN 16:13 NCV

He who searches our hearts knows the mind of the Spirit, because the Spirit intercedes for the saints in accordance with God's will.
ROMANS 8:27 NIV

My Will

Respect Rules

My Own,

I have created you and desire for you to be a citizen of My kingdom. However, this does not mean that you should ignore earthly rules. Of course, I want you to place My rules above all others—to love Me with your whole heart and love others as you love yourself. But after that, I desire that you submit yourself to the authorities that rule and serve on this earth.

Some of those in authority are flawed, and some laws aren't written in wisdom. But for the most part, the system in place is better than no system at all. And as you learn to submit to Me, I want you also to submit to those whom I have placed over you. I can use parents, teachers, law officers, and others to play a significant role in your life. Trust Me and allow Me to take control of the person you are.

So respect authority as you respect Me and even go a step further; pray for those in leadership over you. Pray that they will walk with Me and learn to be better rulers.

With all authority,

The Ruler of All

MATTHEW 22:21 NIV

Then he said to them, "Give to Caesar what is Caesar's, and to God what is God's."

> "Remind your people to obey the government and its officers, and always to be obedient and ready for any honest work."
>
> TITUS 3:1 TLB

Submit yourselves to every ordinance of man for the Lord's sake, whether to the king as supreme, or to governors. . . . For this is the will of God, that by doing good you may put to silence the ignorance of foolish men—as free, yet not using liberty as a cloak for vice, but as bondservants of God. Honor all people. Love the brotherhood. Fear God. Honor the king.
1 PETER 2:13-17 NKJV

JEREMIAH 3:15 TLB

I will give you leaders after my own heart, who will guide you with wisdom and understanding.

Obey those who rule over you, and be submissive, for they watch out for your souls, as those who must give account. Let them do so with joy and not with grief, for that would be unprofitable for you.
HEBREWS 13:17 NKJV

Servants, obey your earthly masters in every way, not as men-pleasers when working under their eyes, but with unmixed motives out of reverence for the Lord. Whatever you do, work heartily as for the Lord and not for men, for you know that from the Lord you will receive a reward of the inheritance. It is Christ the Lord for whom you are working.
COLOSSIANS 3:22-24 MLB

Authority

The Big Liar

My Own,

As you know, I don't give My enemy too much attention, but I need to warn you that he, above all else, is a horrible liar. Without doubt, deception is his favorite weapon to use against those who love Me. I don't want you to be tricked by his cruel deceit.

Satan's lies are never obvious; he's much smarter than that. In fact, he usually mixes a little truth with each lie. For instance, he might make you think that My love results from your performance—that if you're not good enough or if you somehow blow it, I will stop loving you. Ha! Nothing could be further from the truth! My love for you is unconditional. But the morsel of truth in that whopper is, when you step away from Me in sin, you may feel that I don't love you. That's what Satan, who is also known as the father of lies, wants you to believe. And if you already feel badly, it can sound pretty believable.

So watch out! Learn to be wary of his tricky ways. Come to Me with everything, for I can show you what is true and what is not.

In all honesty,

Your One True God

HEBREWS 2:18 NKJV

In that He Himself has suffered, being tempted, He is able to aid those who are tempted.

174

> " Be of sober spirit, be on the alert. Your adversary, the devil, prowls around like a roaring lion, seeking someone to devour. But resist him, firm in your faith, knowing that the same experiences of suffering are being accomplished by your brethren who are in the world. "
>
> I PETER 5:8-9 NAS

No temptation has seized you except what is common to man. And God is faithful; he will not let you be tempted beyond what you can bear. But when you are tempted, he will also provide a way out so that you can stand up under it.

1 CORINTHIANS 10:13 NIV

PSALM 41:12 TLB

You have preserved me because I was honest; you have admitted me forever to your presence.

The great dragon was cast out, that serpent of old, called the Devil and Satan, who deceives the whole world; he was cast to the earth, and his angels were cast out with him.

REVELATION 12:9 NKJV

Kings take pleasure in honest lips; they value a man who speaks the truth.

PROVERBS 16:13 NIV

I know, my God, that you search the heart, and take pleasure in uprightness.

1 CHRONICLES 29:17 NRSV

Truth

Lonely, Not Alone

My Own,

Everyone gets lonely sometimes. The odd thing is that when you feel particularly lonely, you begin to believe you're the only one who feels that way. This is just another one of Satan's lies. The truth is that all humans experience loneliness from time to time.

A part of the human spirit longs for companionship but is never completely satisfied by the company of another person, at least not over an extended period of time. That's where I come in, My friend, for only I can satisfy that deepest longing for companionship. Only I can fulfill that strong desire for intimate fellowship.

The good news is that I am always available to you. Even if you feel lonely, you need to remember you are never alone. I am ready and eager to spend time with you. Just ask. I'm here.

Always waiting,

Your Very Best Friend

JAMES 4:8 NKJV

Draw near to God and He will draw near to you.

"Look! I have been standing at the door and I am constantly knocking. If anyone hears me calling him and opens the door, I will come in and fellowship with him and he with me."

REVELATION 3:20 TLB

The LORD says, "This is my agreement with these people: My Spirit and my words that I give you will never leave you or your children or your grandchildren, now and forever."
ISAIAH 59:21 NCV

And teaching them to obey everything I have commanded you. And surely I am with you always, to the very end of the age.
MATTHEW 28:20 NIV

I JOHN 1:3 NKJV

That which we have seen and heard we declare to you, that you also may have fellowship with us; and truly our fellowship is with the Father and with His Son Jesus Christ.

O LORD, You know; remember me and visit me, and take vengeance for me on my persecutors. In Your enduring patience, do not take me away.
JEREMIAH 15:15 NKJV

I Am with You

> **The LORD replied, "My Presence will go with you, and I will give you rest."**
>
> EXODUS 33:14 NIV

He is close to all who call on him sincerely.
PSALM 145:18 TLB

If I take the wings of the dawn, If I dwell in the remotest part of the sea, Even there Your hand will lead me, And Your right hand will lay hold of me.
PSALM 139:9-10 NAS

You are My friends if you do whatever I command you. No longer do I call you servants, for a servant does not know what his master is doing; but I have called you friends, for all things that I heard from My Father I have made known to you.
JOHN 15:14-15 NKJV

See, I am sending an angel ahead of you to guard you along the way and to bring you to the place I have prepared.
EXODUS 23:20 NIV

❝I will ask the Father, and he will give you another Counselor, who will never leave you. ❞

JOHN 14:16 NLT

The LORD himself goes before you and will be with you; he will never leave you nor forsake you. Do not be afraid; do not be discouraged.
DEUTERONOMY 31:8 NIV

Then we will never forsake you again. Revive us so we can call on your name once more.
PSALM 80:18 NLT

PROVERBS 3:3 NIV

Let love and faithfulness never leave you; bind them around your neck, write them on the tablet of your heart.

I am convinced that neither death nor life, neither angels nor authorities, neither present nor future affairs, neither powers of the heights nor of the depths, nor anything else created will be able to separate us from the love of God that is in Christ Jesus our Lord.
ROMANS 8:38-39 MLB

I Am with You

Rock Solid

Dear Loved One,

You live in a constantly changing world, which is moving faster all the time. It can feel overwhelming and unstable. Sometimes it might even seem that you can't get a firm foothold and are in danger of stumbling and falling.

But I am your solid Rock, My friend. I will never move away or change. By My nature, I am constant and dependable, and you can confidently build your life on Me. Just like a wise man who builds his house on a rock foundation rather than a sandy one, you will not be destroyed when life's storms roll in—you will be firmly grounded in Me.

You might experience some shaking and trembling as the wind and waves howl and crash around you, but when it's all over, you will still be safe and secure and steady, planted on the Rock that never moves.

Steadfast and sure,

Your Rock to Stand On

2 THESSALONIANS 3:3
NKJV

The Lord is faithful, who will establish you and guard you from the evil one.

> **Everyone who hears these words of mine and puts them into practice is like a wise man who built his house on the rock.**

MATTHEW 7:24 NIV

The Lord is my fort where I can enter and be safe; no one can follow me in and slay me. He is a rugged mountain where I hide; he is my Savior, a rock where none can reach me, and a tower of safety. He is my shield. He is like the strong horn of a mighty fighting bull.
PSALM 18:2 TLB

PSALM 18:31 NLT

Who but our God is a solid rock?

He only is my rock and my salvation, my stronghold; I shall not be shaken. On God my salvation and my glory rest; the rock of my strength, my refuge is in God.
PSALM 62:6-7 NAS

You are my hiding place; You preserve me from trouble.
PSALM 32:7 NAS

Our Lord is great and very powerful. There is no limit to what he knows.
PSALM 147:5 NCV

Foundation

The happiness of this
world will fade away.

Real Happiness

Dear Loved One,

One of the most sought-after things on earth is happiness. I watch as people run here and there, chasing after the pleasures of this world, desperately trying, if only for a moment, to catch just a single ray of happiness. But the happiness of this world is slippery and fleeting.

That's not so with My happiness. My happiness is abundant and lasting and real, and I'm ready to share it with all My children. I want to share it with you.

But first you must understand that My happiness is more than just feeling good or experiencing pleasure. My happiness doesn't promise "all fun and games," although I like seeing My children have a good time. My happiness delivers a deeply rooted sense of contentment and satisfaction that remains intact despite your problems and difficulties. My happiness can make you smile when others are ready to curse. It can sustain you through the trials of life with a cheerful heart. Come to Me to find real happiness!

Happily yours,

Your Fulfillment

PROVERBS 16:20 TLB

God blesses those who obey him; happy the man who puts his trust in the Lord.

> **Trust in the LORD, and do good; dwell in the land, and feed on His faithfulness.**
>
> PSALM 37:3 NKJV

All the days of the oppressed are wretched, but the cheerful heart has a continual feast.
PROVERBS 15:15 NIV

I conclude that, first, there is nothing better for a man than to be happy and to enjoy himself as long as he can.
ECCLESIASTES 3:12 TLB

JAMES 1:12 TLB

Happy is the man who doesn't give in and do wrong when he is tempted, for afterwards he will get as his reward the crown of life that God has promised those who love him.

Let all who take refuge in You be glad, let them ever sing for joy; and may You shelter them, that those who love Your name may exult in Thee.
PSALM 5:11 NAS

Serving God does make us very rich, if we are satisfied with what we have. We brought nothing into the world, so we can take nothing out. But, if we have food and clothes, we will be satisfied with that.
1 TIMOTHY 6:6-8 NCV

Happiness

> **"Wisdom is a tree of life to those who eat her fruit; happy is the man who keeps on eating it."**
>
> PROVERBS 3:18 TLB

To him who is able to keep you from falling and to present you before his glorious presence without fault and with great joy.
JUDE 24 NIV

Praise the Lord!
For all who fear God and trust in him are blessed beyond expression.
Yes, happy is the man who delights in doing his commands.
PSALM 112:1 TLB

I have said these things to you so that my joy may be in you, and that your joy may be complete.
JOHN 15:11 NRSV

You will show me the way of life, granting me the joy of your presence and the pleasures of living with you forever.
PSALM 16:11 NLT

Blessed are the pure in heart, for they will see God. Blessed are the peacemakers, for they will be called children of God.
MATTHEW 5:8-9 NRSV

> **"At last I shall be fully satisfied; I will praise you with great joy."**
>
> PSALM 63:5 TLB

I will go to the altar of God, to God who is my joy and happiness. I will praise you with a harp, God, my God.
PSALM 43:4 NCV

His master replied, "Well done, good and faithful servant! You have been faithful with a few things; I will put you in charge of many things. Come and share your master's happiness!"
MATTHEW 25:23 NIV

I PETER 1:8 NCV

You have not seen Christ, but still you love him. You cannot see him now, but you believe in him. So you are filled with a joy that cannot be explained, a joy full of glory.

Give great joy to those who have stood with me in my defense. Let them continually say, "Great is the LORD, who enjoys helping his servant."
PSALM 35:27 NLT

Happy are those whose help is the God of Jacob, whose hope is in the LORD their God.
PSALM 146:5 NRSV

A tranquil mind gives life to the flesh, but passion makes the bones rot.
PROVERBS 14:30 NRSV

Happiness

Forever Promise

One Whom I Love,

Eternity is a long, long time. Your earthly mind can't even begin to fathom its mysteries, although your spirit sometimes whispers of immortality and of life beyond this life. I know you sense there's more to this world than what you see with your eyes. And so there is.

But how can I explain the limitless dimensions of eternity except to say that I hold it all in My hands, just as I hold you in My hands. It is all under control, My perfect control. You must learn to trust Me for what is unknown.

Believe Me, eternity is absolutely magnificent, extraordinary, fantastic even! Living forever with Me in My incredible kingdom will be much, much more than you've ever dreamed and far greater than anything you can ever imagine!

And did you know that it begins right now? For you experience eternity each time you experience My love, My presence in your life, My touch upon your heart. With your hand in Mine, we're walking in eternity now! That's exciting. You and I, and eternity, forever and ever. Amen!

Eternally yours,

The Lord
God Almighty

JOHN 3:16 NIV

For God so loved the world that he gave his one and only Son, that whoever believes in him shall not perish but have eternal life.

187

> **"Jesus said to her, 'I am the resurrection and the life; he who believes in Me will live even if he dies, and everyone who lives and believes in Me will never die. Do you believe this?'"**
>
> JOHN 11:25-26 NAS

This is the testimony: that God has given us eternal life, and this life is in His Son. He who has the Son has life; he who does not have the Son of God does not have life. These things I have written to you who believe in the name of the Son of God, that you may know that you have eternal life, and that you may continue to believe in the name of the Son of God.
1 JOHN 5:11-13 NKJV

1 JOHN 2:25 NLT

In this fellowship we enjoy the eternal life he promised us.

Being justified by His grace we would be made heirs according to the hope of eternal life.
TITUS 3:7 NAS

I will display my greatness and my holiness and make myself known in the eyes of many nations. Then they shall know that I am the LORD.
EZEKIEL 38:23 NRSV

Eternity

> **"Keep yourselves in the love of God; look forward to the mercy of our Lord Jesus Christ that leads to eternal life."**
>
> JUDE 21 NRSV

All who trust him—God's Son—to save them have eternal life; those who don't believe and obey him shall never see heaven, but the wrath of God remains upon them.
JOHN 3:36 TLB

Since death came through a man, the resurrection of the dead comes also through a man.
1 CORINTHIANS 15:21 NIV

Surely goodness and mercy shall follow me all the days of my life; and I will dwell in the house of the LORD forever.
PSALM 23:6 NKJV

The water I give them takes away thirst altogether. It becomes a perpetual spring within them, giving them eternal life.
JOHN 4:14 NLT

I am about to create new heavens and a new earth; the former things shall not be remembered or come to mind.
ISAIAH 65:17 NRSV

Forever Promise

> **"This is what God has testified: He has given us eternal life, and this life is in his Son."**
>
> 1 JOHN 5:11 NLT

He died for all so that all who live—having received eternal life from him—might live no longer for themselves, to please themselves, but to spend their lives pleasing Christ who died and rose again for them.
2 CORINTHIANS 5:15 TLB

All who believe in God's Son have eternal life. Those who don't obey the Son will never experience eternal life, but the wrath of God remains upon them.
JOHN 3:36 NLT

JOHN 5:24 NAS

Truly, truly, I say to you, he who hears My word, and believes Him who sent Me, has eternal life, and does not come into judgment, but has passed out of death into life.

Now that you have been set free from sin and have become slaves to God, the benefit you reap leads to holiness, and the result is eternal life.
ROMANS 6:22 NIV

There will never be night again. They will not need the light of a lamp or the light of the sun, because the Lord God will give them light. And they will rule as kings forever and ever.
REVELATION 22:5 NCV

Eternity

If you have enjoyed this book, you will also enjoy other gift books available from your local bookstore.

Letters from God
Daily Blessings for My Husband
Daily Blessings for My Wife
Daily Blessings for My Secret Pal
Lighthouse Psalms
Garden Psalms
Love Psalms
Psalms for Women

If this book has impacted your life, we would like to hear from you.

Please contact us at:

Honor Books
Department E
P.O. Box 55388
Tulsa, Oklahoma 74155

Or by e-mail at:
info@honorbooks.com

LETTERS from GOD for TEENS

love   forgiven

prayer   friend

shine   roman

knowing   doir

peace   accept

waiting   blues